THE SHAPING OF
THE MODERN MIDDLE EAST

The Arabs in History (1950, new ed. 1993)

The Emergence of Modern Turkey (1961, rev. ed. 1968)

Istanbul and the Civilization of the Ottoman Empire (1963)

The Assassins (1968)

The Muslim Discovery of Europe (1982)

The Jews of Islam (1984)

The Political Language of Islam (1988)

*Race and Slavery in the Middle East:
An Historical Enquiry* (1990)

Islam in History (1993)

Islam and the West (1993)

THE SHAPING OF
THE MODERN
MIDDLE EAST

Bernard Lewis

New York   Oxford
OXFORD UNIVERSITY PRESS
1994

Oxford University Press

Oxford   New York   Toronto
Delhi   Bombay   Calcutta   Madras   Karachi
Kuala Lumpur   Singapore   Hong Kong   Tokyo
Nairobi   Dar es Salaam   Cape Town
Melbourne   Auckland   Madrid

and associated companies in
Berlin   Ibadan

Published by Oxford University Press, Inc.,
200 Madison Avenue, New York, New York 10016

Oxford is a registered trademark of Oxford University Press

Library of Congress Cataloging-in-Publication Data
Lewis, Bernard
The shaping of the modern Middle East / Bernard Lewis.
p. cm.   Includes index.
ISBN 0-19-507281-2—ISBN 0-19-507282-0 (pbk.)
1. Middle East—History—1517—   I. Title.
DS62.4.L48   1994
956—dc20   93–3283

2 4 6 8 9 7 5 3 1

Printed in the United States of America
on acid-free paper

~~~~~~~~~~

Preface

The nucleus of this book is a series of six public lectures delivered at Indiana University, Bloomington, between 19 March and 23 April 1963. Their theme is the relations between the Middle East and the West—the impact of both Western action and Western civilization on the Islamic peoples and societies of the Middle East, and the successive phases of Middle Eastern response. In the first chapter I have attempted to define the Middle East as a historical, geographical, and cultural entity; in the second, to show what the West has meant and means to Middle Easterners and to trace the processes of Western intrusion, influence, domination, and partial withdrawal. The next three chapters deal with political and intellectual movements in the Middle East in recent and modern times, in three main groups—liberal and socialist, patriotic and nationalist, and Islamic. The final chapter examines the place and role of the countries of the Middle East in international affairs and concludes with a consideration of some of the factors affecting Western policy toward them.

During the nearly thirty years that have passed since the delivery and publication of these lectures, vast changes have taken place in both the world and the region. The Cold War flared to a climax, inflamed the Middle East, and ended. The Soviet Union itself disintegrated, and the vast Muslim lands that had been conquered by the czars and incorporated into the Russian empire recovered their independence and seemed to be returning to the historic Middle East of which they had once been a part. Arabs and Israelis fought several more wars. Palestinians, despairing of active help from the Arab states, formed their own organization. An Egyptian statesman initiated and accomplished the first peace treaty between Israel and an Arab state, and a process was begun which might in time lead to a more general peace in the region. A dictator in Iraq invaded and annexed a neighboring Arab state, thus flouting the rules of both inter-Arab and international coexistence and provoking a massive intervention and involvement of the United States. A revolution in Iran evoked responses all over the Middle East and indeed all over the Islamic world, and transformed the region through the emergence of a new regional power and a new Islamic ideology, radical in both its objectives and its methods.

In all three major themes examined in the lectures—religion, nationhood, and the quest for freedom—far-reaching and significant changes took place, including both successes and failures, both the return to old traditions and the pursuit of new ideas.

In this new edition, I have tried to present and interpret the major changes that have taken place, the new perceptions of freedom, both national and personal, and the attempts being made to achieve it, the changing content and significance of national and patriotic loyalties, and the resurgence of religious and communal identities and commitments. In discussing these processes, I have tried to situate them in both a global and a regional context—in the shifting interplay of regional and global powers on the one hand, and in the far-reaching changes in Middle Eastern economies and societies on the other.

The study of recent and contemporary history presents special problems to the historian. There is the obvious difficulty of the fragmentary and usually secondary quality of his documentation, but in compensation there is the immediacy of his experience of the events of his own time. This in turn brings another danger—that of the historian's own involvement and commitments. We are all, including historians, the children of our own time and place, with loyalties, or at least predispositions, determined by country, race, gender, religion, ideology, and economic, social, and cultural background. Some have argued that since complete impartiality is impossible, the historian should abandon the attempt as false and hypocritical, and present himself frankly as a partisan of his cause. If his cause is just, according to this view, his story will to that degree be authentic. If his cause is unjust, his story will be flawed and should be dismissed accordingly.

In this book, I have adhered to a different view: that the historian owes it to himself and to his readers to try, to the best of his ability, to be objective or at least to be fair—to be conscious of his own commitments and concerns and make due allowance and, where necessary, correct for them, to try to present the different aspects of a problem and the different sides to a dispute in such a way as to allow the reader to form an independent judgment. Above all, he should not prejudge issues and predetermine results by the arbitrary selection of evidence and the use of emotionally charged or biased language. As a famous economist once remarked, "Complete asepsis is impossible, but one does not for that reason perform surgery in a sewer."

The reader will judge how far I have succeeded in my antiseptic precautions to avoid infection. I derive some reassurance from the reception of the first edition of this book, which, among other languages, was translated and published in both Hebrew and Arabic. The Hebrew version was sponsored by the publishing house of the Israeli Ministry of Defense, the Arabic version by the Muslim Brothers. The Arabic translation appeared in two editions: a full book-length version and a shortened version in pamphlet form that was hawked in the vicinity of mosques. I hope I may be forgiven for feeling that a presentation which both Israeli Defense officials and Muslim Brothers thought worthy of publication under their auspices may have achieved some level of objectivity. The translator of the Arabic version, in his introductory remarks, observes that the author of this book is one of two things: a candid friend or an honorable enemy, and in either case, one who does not distort or evade the truth. I am content to abide by that judgment.

Princeton, N.J.   B.L.
April 1993

~~~~~~~~~~

Acknowledgments

The earlier version of this book contained the following note of ac-knowledgment:

> I should like to record my thanks to Indiana University for giving me this opportunity to present my views on this subject, and to my colleagues and students at Bloomington for their gracious and friendly hospitality during the six weeks of my stay. My thanks are also due to my colleagues Dr. S. A. A. Rizvi and Dr. M. E. Yapp, for several helpful suggestions, and to Professor A. T. Hatto and Mr. E. Kedourie for reading and criticizing my typescript. They are of course in no way responsible for any defects that remain. Finally, I would like to thank Professor W. Cantwell Smith and the New American Library of World Literature Inc., for permission to re-produce the passage cited on p. 168, and Simon and Schuster for a quotation from James G. McDonald's *My Mission to Israel*.

It is now my very pleasant duty to thank my assistant, Jane Baun, for her invaluable help in preparing—and in many different ways, improving—this new edition. I should also like to record my indebtedness to Nancy Lane and Irene Pavitt, of Oxford University Press, for their help and advice in the production of this book. Once again, I offer my thanks to all of them for their many suggestions that I accepted, and my apologies for those that I resisted. From this it will be clear that whatever defects remain are entirely my own.

Contents

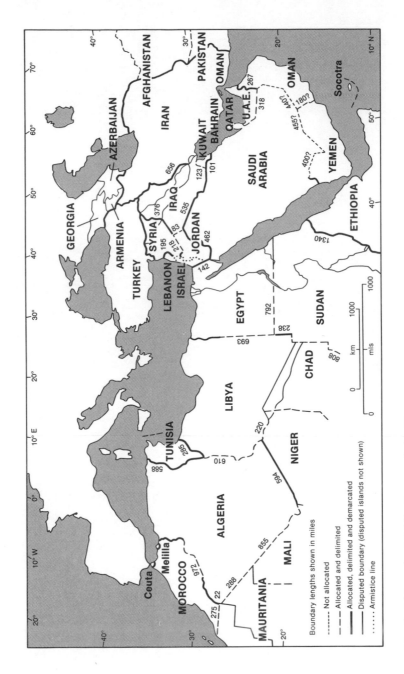

North Africa, the Middle East, and the Caucasus

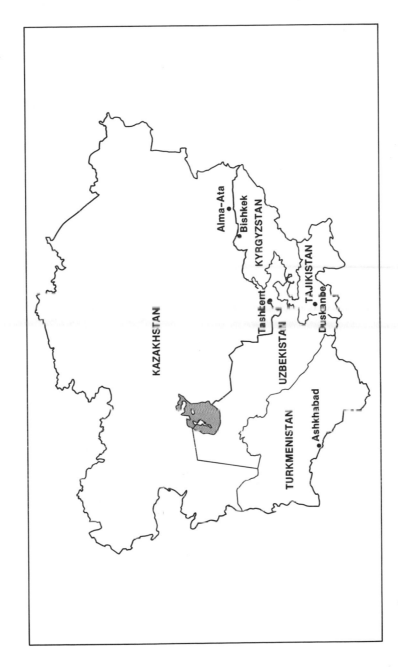

Central Asia

THE SHAPING OF
THE MODERN MIDDLE EAST

1

~~~~~~~~~~

Sketches for a
Historical Portrait

The term "Middle East" was invented in 1902 by the American naval historian Alfred Thayer Mahan, to designate the area between Arabia and India, with its center—from the point of view of the naval strategist—in the Persian Gulf. This new geographical expression was taken up by *The Times* (of London) and later by the British government and, together with the slightly earlier term "Near East," soon passed into general use. Both names are recent but not modern; both are relics of a world with Western Europe in the center and other regions grouped around it. Yet in spite of their obsolete origin and parochial outlook, both terms, "Middle East" in particular, have won universal acceptance and are now used to designate this region even by Russians, Africans, and Indians, for whom in fact it lies south, north, or west—even, strangest of all, by the peoples of the Middle East themselves. So useful has the term been found to be that the area of its application, as well as of its use, has been vastly extended, from the original coastlands of the Persian Gulf to a broad region stretching from the Black Sea to equatorial Africa and from the northwest frontier of India to the Atlantic.[1]

It is indeed remarkable that a region of such ancient civilization—among the most ancient in the world—should have come to be known, even to itself, by names that are so new and so colorless. Yet if we try to find an adequate substitute for these names, we shall have great difficulty. In India the attempt has indeed been made

3

to displace the Western-centered term "Middle East" by another, and the area has been renamed "Western Asia." This new geographical expression has rather more shape and color than "Middle East," but is not really very much better. It is no less misleading to view the region as the West of an entity called Asia than as the Middle East of another unspecified entity; moreover, it is misleading to designate it by a name that, even formally, excludes Egypt.

The reason for the rapid spread and acceptance of the terms "Near East" and "Middle East" must be sought in the fact that for Europeans this region was, for millennia, *the* East—the classical, archetypal, and immemorial Orient which had been the neighbor and rival of Greco-Roman and Christian Europe from the days when the armies of the Great King of Persia first invaded the lands of the Greeks until the days when the last rearguards of the Ottoman sultans withdrew. Well into the nineteenth century, the countries of Southwest Asia and Northeastern Africa were, for the European, still simply The East, without any need for closer specification, and the problem of their disposal was the Eastern Question. It was only when Europe became involved in the problems of a vaster and more remote Orient that a closer definition became necessary. When the Far East began to concern the chanceries of Europe, some separate designation of the nearer east was needed. The term "Near East" was originally applied in the late nineteenth century to that part of southeastern Europe that was then still under Turkish rule. It was "Near" because it was, after all, Christian and European; it was "East" because it was still under the rule of the Ottoman Empire— of an Islamic and "Eastern" state. For a while, the Near East was, so to speak, extended eastward and, especially in American usage, came to embrace the greater part of the territories of the Ottoman Empire, in Asia and Africa as well as in Europe. In British usage— perhaps because on closer acquaintance the Near East proved less near than had at first been thought—the term "Near East" has almost disappeared and has been replaced by a vastly extended Middle East covering large areas of Southwest Asia and North Africa. There is still considerable variation in the usage of the latter term.

In spite of its recent emergence and a continuing uncertainty as to its precise location, the term "Middle East" does nevertheless designate an area with an unmistakable character and identity, a distinctive—and familiar—personality shaped by strong geographical features and by a long and famous history.

The most striking geographical characteristic of the Middle East is certainly its aridity—the vast expanses of wasteland in almost every part of it. Rainfall is sparse, forests are few, and, except for a few privileged areas, agriculture depends on perennial irrigation and requires constant defense against natural and human erosion. Most of the Arabian peninsula, apart from its southwestern and southeastern corners, consists of desert; the Fertile Crescent is little more than a rim of irrigable and cultivable land around its northern edges. Egypt, too, is nearly all desert, save only for the green gash of the Nile, opening out into the delta toward the shore of the Mediterranean Sea. Much of North Africa is now infertile, except for the coastal belt and a few oases. In Turkey and Iran, much of the central plateau consists of desert and steppe, while beyond them, to the north, lie the vast steppelands of Eurasia.

Some of the deserts, as in the Empty Quarter of Arabia and the Western Desert of Egypt, are utterly barren; others support a thin but historically important population of nomadic herdsmen who provide animals for meat, milk, and transport and participate, in various ways, in the exploitation of the transdesert trade routes. In modern times, the herdsmen are losing an important part of their economic *raison d'être* as horse and camel are replaced by car and truck—mounts that they are unable to breed. They can, however, feed them, and in some areas they and their neighbors are supplied with vast quantities of the fodder that these mounts consume. The exploitation of this resource—petroleum—is bringing social as well as economic changes of incalculable scope and extent.

The impact of the discovery and exploitation of oil in the Middle East was dramatic, in that this was a region previously deficient in sources of fuel and energy. There was no coal, and even in the Middle Ages, there was very little wood, so that leather and wool—products of the nomads—were used for both furnishings and clothes. The presence of oil was known, but its potential was not realized. In pre-Islamic Iran, it was used to maintain the sacred flame in Zoroastrian temples; in Islamic times, it was an ingredient in the manufacture of explosive mixtures for use as weapons of war. Apart from water and windmills—and these few in number as compared with even early medieval Europe—there was no energy source beyond animal and human strength. This may also help explain the lack of technological progress after the remarkable achievements in this respect of Middle Eastern antiquity.

Between the herdsmen and the tillers of the soil there is an ancient feud. One of the earliest records of the conflict between them is contained in some verses of the fourth chapter of the book of Genesis, which tells of the quarrel of Abel, the stockraiser, and

Cain, the farmer. In the Bible it is Cain who kills Abel; more frequently in the history of the Middle East it has been the herdsmen who killed the peasants or established their rule over them. The policing of the desert borders and the security of the desert trade routes were always problems for the governments, whether local or imperial, that controlled the settled country. They usually found it more convenient to deal with the desert by indirect means, through some sort of nomadic or oasis principality to which they gave support and recognition in return for commercial facilities and political and military help when required. To take one example among many: Byzantium and Persia, the two world powers that confronted each other across the Middle East in the sixth and early seventh centuries, both maintained their Arabian buffer states, whose rulers they encouraged with gifts of gold and of weapons, high-sounding titles, and visits to the imperial capital. This method was cheaper, easier, and more effective than trying to rule the desert directly. Its merits are in no way diminished by the fact that in the seventh century the Arabs came out of the desert and overwhelmed both of them.

Conquest from the desert is a recurring theme in the history of the Middle East. Many waves of invasion, migration, and settlement have burst into the cultivated lands. Some, like those of the Accadians, the Canaanites, the Aramaeans, and the Hebrews in antiquity, were of Semitic peoples from the Arabian wilderness; others came southward from the steppelands of Central, northern, and eastern Asia. The last and greatest of the Semitic invasions was that of the Muslim Arabs in the seventh century, which inaugurated medieval Islamic civilization; the greatest of the steppe invasions was that of the Mongols in the thirteenth century, who, in the judgment of some historians, ended it.

The immediate impact of the Mongol conquests was certainly great, but their subsequent effects have been much exaggerated. At one time, Mongol brutality was blamed for the decline of Islamic civilization and, indeed, for all the failings of the Middle East and its peoples between the thirteenth and nineteenth centuries. Outside romantic and apologetic circles, this view has been generally abandoned, as increased knowledge of Islamic history, on the one hand, and closer experience of brutality and destruction, on the other, have shown us that the damage done by the Mongols was neither as great nor as lasting as it seemed to historians of a more innocent age than our own. The Mongols did not destroy Arab civilization, which had passed its prime long before they appeared; nor did they destroy

Islamic civilization, which, in a predominantly Persianized form, achieved a new flowering under their rule.

But Islamic civilization, though not destroyed, was undoubtedly transformed by the coming of the steppe peoples. The great migrations of these peoples into the Middle East had begun before the Mongol conquests, in the tenth century, when the Turkish tribes of Central Asia crossed the Jaxartes and began their march of conquest westward. They ended in the period after the death of Tamerlane, the last of the great steppe conquerors, in 1405. During these four centuries of invasion and domination from the steppe, the whole pattern of life and government in the Middle East was changed.

Thereafter, there were no more invasions from the desert or the steppe. When the Wahhābīs in eighteenth-century Arabia, moved by a new religious fervor and a new expansionist drive, tried to emulate the feats of their ancestors by invading Syria and Iraq, they were stopped on the desert borders and hurled back. The Ottoman Empire, then in the last stages of decrepitude, succeeded with ease where the mighty empires of Rome and Persia had failed. The difference was, of course, the technological superiority of the stronger power over the weaker, which began with the advent of the first firearm and has been growing ever since. The Persian and Byzantine armies faced the desert invaders with weapons little, if at all, better than those of their enemies; the Ottomans stopped them with guns.

Here and there the desert is broken by rivers, which can be used for irrigation. Two of the most important countries, Egypt and Iraq, are essentially river valleys. Both have societies of great antiquity—certainly the most ancient in the area, perhaps in the world. Both have agrarian economies based on elaborate artificial irrigation, using the floodwater of the rivers and requiring large numbers of workers and of skilled technicians, controlled by a central administrative authority. This need determined the evolution of the system of land tenure; it also encouraged the growth of strong, centralized governments, at once bureaucratic and autocratic, and of a corresponding tradition of political thought and behavior.

The rich harvests of the irrigated river valleys produced more than was needed for simple subsistence and made possible a level of specialization previously unknown and the development of new skills and enterprises. Already during the fourth millennium B.C., the city dwellers of Iraq and Egypt organized trade by land and sea to bring them the timber and minerals that they lacked. No less significant was the invention of writing. The growth of the cities, of temple and palace stores, and of a form of government required some system of accounts and records. To meet this need, the specialized "mystery" of writing came into being and, with it, a new social class of scribes and clerks and the revolutionary possibility of recording, accumulating, and transmitting knowledge.

Most of the oldest urban centers and the earliest written records known to mankind come from the Middle East. Later, both urbanism and writing were transformed by the contributions of many peoples inside and outside the region. The Phoenician alphabet, replacing the complicated pictorial and syllabic scripts of the ancient Egyptians and Babylonians, enormously facilitated and accelerated the development of writing. The Greek *polis*, with its participating citizens and its inquiring thinkers and scientists, opened new paths in the culture and government of cities. At the time of the advent of Islam in the seventh century A.D., North Africa, Egypt, the Levant, and Asia Minor had for centuries been under Greco-Roman rule or influence, and such great cities as Alexandria, Caesarea, Antioch, and Constantinople were centers of Hellenistic civilization.

The older cities of the interior—Thebes, Jerusalem, Damascus—though also subject to Hellenistic influence, preserved an older Middle Eastern tradition. This tradition was still stronger in Iraq, which, although by that time largely Christian, was not incorporated into the Greco-Roman world but was a part—and indeed the metropolitan province—of the Persian Empire. The Islamic world created by the Arab conquerors united, for the first time since Alexander the Great and for a much longer period, both the eastern and western parts of the Middle Eastern region and included the river valleys and ancient centers of both Egypt and Iraq.

These two have for millennia been rival centers of power, and their modes of thought and organization have profoundly influenced the neighboring countries. It was from these centers that, in remote antiquity, civilization first arose and spread in the Middle East, in these centers again that, after the long eclipse from Cyrus to Muḥammad, the new imperial civilization of Islam was born and grew to greatness. Since the Middle Ages, Egypt has, by superior numbers and economic resources, decisively outstripped Iraq, although the wealth accruing to the latter from oil sometimes obscures but does not remove this inequality.

Egypt and Iraq have not always been the rival masters of the Middle East. There have been other centers of power in the area, the seats of empires that for long periods dominated the more ancient

lands. North and east of the plains and valleys that make up the
Fertile Crescent lie the great, high plateaus of Iran and Anatolia,
clearly marked off from them in geographical configuration, population, cultural tradition, and political experience. These lands were
greatly influenced by the Semitic civilizations of the Fertile Crescent, in both their ancient and their Islamic flowerings. But although
they have passed through many ethnic and linguistic changes and
adopted several Semitic scripts, they never adopted Semitic speech.
Persians in the east and Hittites, Greeks, and Turks in the north
have stood on roughly the same ethnic boundaries. Ottomans and
Safavids in the sixteenth century resumed the roles and conflicts of
Byzantines and Sasanids in the sixth, and evoked still more ancient
memories. Today the tablelands form the two states of Turkey and
Iran, inhabited by peoples who, though Muslim, share neither the
language of the Arabs nor the long trauma of subjection and liberation. The dividing line between Arab and non-Arab is an old one,
and the frontier that it marks, along the foothills and the mountain
approaches, is much older.

Between Taurus and Sinai, between the desert and the sea, lies
the region forming the four modern states of Syria, Lebanon, Israel,
and Jordan, which the Greeks and Romans called Syria, the Arabs
called the lands of Shām, and European traders called the Levant.
The broken terrain of this region is in marked contrast with the
river valleys and plateaus that supported the neighboring empires
and has usually been reflected in a cultural and political fragmen
tation. Only on rare occasions has the temporary eclipse of other
powers permitted the emergence of a strong power in Syria. More
often, the Syrian lands formed a mosaic of small principalities, the
objects and the scene of struggles between their more powerful
neighbors. When the rulers of Egypt were strong, it was they who
tried to extend their control into as much of Syria as possible, as
did Pharaoh Thutmosis and Ptolemy, Pompey and Ibn Tūlūn, Fa-
timids and Mamluks, Napoleon, Muhammad 'Alī, the British, and
Nasser. Egypt is most vulnerable on its northeastern frontier,
through which many invaders have come, and Egyptian governments have usually tried to maintain at least a bridgehead on the
far side of Sinai. At other times, the Levant was dominated from
the east—for example, by the Assyrians, the Persians, and the Ab-
basids; from the north—by the Hittites, Byzantines, and Ottomans;
or from the sea.

A dominant geographical feature of this region is the spine of
mountains that runs down its center—the Lebanon and Anti-

Lebanon, with their northward and southward extensions. The mountains divide the Syrian lands into two: a western slope facing the Mediterranean and Europe, and an eastern slope facing the desert and Asia. The distinction between them is an old one and has from time to time been renewed by fresh waves of invasion from both sides. The Philistines and the Phoenicians were both sea peoples, the former coming from the West, the latter facing toward it. The ancient Israelites were a people of the desert and the hills, who held and finally defeated the Philistine invaders. Greek and Roman culture flourished in the coastlands and languished in the interior. Antioch was a great Greek metropolis, and the maritime city of Berytus housed a notable school of Roman law—the Roman university of Beirut, as it were. Only occasionally, as under the Maccabees in Judea, did the older culture of the interior assert itself against the pervasive Hellenistic influence. The Arab invasions renewed the hegemony of the East and, for a brief interval, even made Damascus an imperial capital. The Crusaders, marching south from Antioch to Gaza, for a while restored the Levant coast to Europe, but could not penetrate the interior. They never entered Aleppo or Damascus and were able to hold Jerusalem, their main objective, for only a short time. In our own day, the distinction between the two is still clear, as between Beirut and Damascus, or, in a different and much more acute form, between Tel Aviv and Amman.

Two hundred years ago, when the European science of Egyptology was just beginning, all that was known of the ancient Middle East before the conquests of Alexander was what was said about it by the Bible and the Greek authors. There were still Egyptians in Egypt, Persians in Persia, the descendants of other ancient peoples in neighboring lands; but the old states and religions and civilizations were dead and literally buried, the old languages long since forgotten, their secrets locked in ancient scripts that no one could decipher. Only a few minorities—Coptic Christians in Egypt and Zoroastrians in Iran and India—remained faithful to the old religions and preserved some knowledge of the final phases of their ancient languages and cultures. These remained unknown outside their own communities. Two of the peoples active in the ancient Middle East had survived with a continuing identity and memory and with a large impact on the world. The Greeks and Jews were still Greeks and Jews and still knew Greek and Hebrew; in these ancient yet living languages, they had preserved immortal works of religion and literature, which passed into the common inheritance of mankind. In these works was all that the living human memory had retained of the ancient Middle East. Even that much was barely known among the Muslims, who read neither the Bible nor the Greek historians and had only a little secondhand information filtered through from these same sources, together with a few vague legends of uncertain origin. The rediscovery of the ancient Middle East was largely the work of European scholarship—of archaeologists who found the sources of information, philologists who, using Coptic and Zoroastrian evidence, deciphered and interpreted them, and historians and others who evaluated and exploited them. Their scholarship ultimately found disciples in the Middle East and added a new dimension to the historical self-awareness of its peoples, which had hitherto in effect been limited to the period beginning with the Islamic revelation.

The Middle East is the home of three great religions: Judaism, Christianity, and Islam. All three of them still survive there; one has prevailed. For the last fourteen centuries, the Middle East has been preeminently the land of Islam, the geographical and spiritual center of the Islamic world, where the Muslim faith was born and the civilization of Islam received its first, classical formulations. Islam is by no means limited to the Middle East, however. There are huge communities of Muslims in Africa and Asia, some of them far larger than the combined population of the Middle East. But all of them are secondary, postclassical, in a sense colonial, related to the heartlands of Islam, as are the lands of overseas settlement to Europe. It was in the Middle East that the great events took place which form the common historical memory of Muslims everywhere, and that the classic Islamic identity evolved. It was there that the basic Islamic patterns and traditions took shape, in the dominions of the caliphs and sultans of the great universal empires of medieval Islam, in lands that were, with some exceptions here and there, of Arabic, Persian, and Turkish speech.

Since the rise of Islam in the seventh century, these three languages have predominated in the region, ousting such earlier media of communication and culture as Greek, Coptic, and Syriac and condemning them either to extinction or to liturgical or dialectal fossilization. The three are very unlike one another, belonging to different and unrelated language families. Arabic is a Semitic language, akin to Hebrew and Syriac; Persian is an Indo-European language, related to Sanskrit on the one side and to most of the languages of Europe on the other; Turkish belongs to another group again, the Turco-Tatar family of languages, extending across Central Asia to the Far East and even to the Arctic. The three languages, though structurally quite different, are culturally closely related; an immense vocabulary of Arabic loanwords is used in Persian, and of Arabic and Persian loanwords in Turkish. Persians and Turks alike drew on Arabic, just as Europeans drew on Latin and Greek, both to borrow existing terms for old notions and to coin new terms for new ones. Both "metaphysics" and "telegraphy" are English words of Greek etymology; the Arabic vocabulary of Turkish offers parallels to both types of borrowing.

The peoples who spoke these three languages appeared successively at the center of the Middle Eastern stage. The first were the Arabs. At the beginning of the seventh century, the Arabs were to be found only in the Arabian peninsula and its borderlands. The many countries in Southwest Asia and North Africa that are now called Arab were inhabited by a variety of nations, most of them Christian by religion, and some, but not all, Semitic in speech. They spoke numerous languages—Aramaic in the Fertile Crescent, Coptic in Egypt, Berber and neo-Punic in North Africa. In addition, they used Greek in the East and Latin in the West as the media of government, commerce, and culture.

As a result of the successive waves of conquest and colonization that followed the rise of Islam in Arabia, these countries were incorporated into a new empire stretching from the Atlantic and the Pyrenees in the West to the borders of China and India in the East. For a couple of centuries, this new empire was dominated by the Arabian conquerors, who formed a sort of conquistador aristocracy within it. The faith that they had brought and the language in which its sacred scriptures were written provided the basis and the medium of a rich new civilization created by people of many faiths and nations, but expressed in the Arabic language and conforming to the standards of Islamic piety and aesthetics. In time, the Arabs were compelled to share or even relinquish their political primacy, giving place to new bureaucratic and military elites of alien origin. The Arabic language, however, retained its cultural preeminence long after its speakers had lost the realities of power. From the border of Persia and Iraq, right across the Fertile Crescent into North Africa, Arabic supplanted all previous official languages and, in its written form, remains the common language to the present day.

East of the Perso-Iraqi border, the Arab conquerors succeeded in imposing their religion, their script, and, for a while, their literary and scientific language, but not their speech or their national identity. The Persians were Islamized; they wrote Arabic and indeed made an enormous contribution to the international literature of

Islam written in the Arabic language. They remained Persian, however, differing from the Arabs in speech and sentiment. Like the other conquered peoples of the Arab Empire, they had an ancient language and literature; unlike them, they were sustained by still recent memories of independence and imperial greatness, and by a practical experience of administration and statecraft that soon won them a leading role in Arab government. During the ninth and tenth centuries, Persia reemerged on the political scene. Independent Persian dynasties appeared in what were formerly provinces of the Arab Empire, and a new Islamic Persian literary language developed with a rich and brilliant literature, responding to the tastes of Persian-speaking courts and patrons and reflecting the new self-awareness of the Persians as a distinct cultural group within Islam—in many ways the most advanced.

From about the tenth century onward, Muslim Persian began to replace Arabic as the predominant literary medium outside the countries of Arabic speech. Arabic was no longer the universal governmental and cultural language of Islam, as Latin had been in medieval Europe. Instead, it was restricted, except for religious and legal purposes, to those countries that, centuries later, came to be called Arab. Farther east, not only in Persia but also in the areas of Persian cultural influence in Turkey, Central Asia, and India, Persian became the dominant literary language, and the Persian replaced the Arabic classics as the models for imitation. As the decline of the Arab lands coincided with the renaissance of Iran, Cairo, Damascus, and Baghdad gave place to the cities of the Persians and Turks, and these became the great creative centers of Islamic civilization, now entering on its second, and Persian, phase of achievement.

At about the same time, or slightly later, the Turks, the third of the three major peoples of the Islamic heartlands, made their appearance. They had come into the Middle East from Central Asia, from their homelands beyond the Jaxartes (Sir Darya) River. Most of the Turks had been pagans, though groups among them had professed forms of Christianity, Manichaeism, Judaism, and Buddhism. But over time they were almost without exception converted to Islam and came to play an important and then, for a long time, a dominant role in the Islamic world.

The Turks at first came into the Middle East as soldiers and individuals and soon predominated in the armies of Islam. In the eleventh century, they came as conquerors and colonists and set up a new empire in the heartlands of Islam, with its center in Persia. The first Arab Muslim conquerors had been halted by the Byzantines at the Taurus Mountains, which from the seventh to the eleventh centuries marked the frontier between Islam and Christendom. The Turks succeeded where earlier invaders had failed, and they pushed the barrier of Europe farther back, bringing Asia Minor into the world of Islam. After the conquest they settled there in great numbers, so that Western visitors—though not the inhabitants—began to call the country Turkey, after the name of the dominant ethnic and linguistic element there.

By conquest and settlement, Asia Minor became a predominantly Turkish land, linked by a continuous belt of Turkish populations with the older Turkish lands in Transcaucasia and Central and eastern Asia. Almost everywhere else in the Middle East, the Turks, though a minority, formed the ruling element. Even in Iran, Syria, and Egypt—even as far away as Muslim India—the ruling dynasties were Turkish, the armies were Turkish, although the overwhelming mass of the population were not. Through a millennium of Turkish hegemony it came to be generally accepted that Turks commanded while others obeyed, and a non-Turk in authority was regarded as an oddity. During this period, Turkish finally emerged as the third major language of the area. Like Persian before it, Turkish was Islamized, written in the Arabic script, with a large Arabo-Persian vocabulary representing the great heritage of Islamic—especially Perso-Islamic—civilization. This language provided the medium of the third great phase of Islamic Middle Eastern civilization, that of the Turks. Its first main center was in the East, where a rich culture flourished in Herat, Samarkand, and Bukhara in the eastern Turkish language. Thereafter, it developed especially in the Ottoman Empire, the last and greatest of the Turkish empires. By the sixteenth century, Ottoman rule, suzerainty, or influence extended over almost all the lands of Arabic speech. Only in a few remote and inaccessible places—in faraway Morocco, the mountain valleys of Lebanon, and the deserts of Arabia—did men of Arabic speech rule themselves. Their return to political independence, after an eclipse of nearly a millennium, has been one of the most explosive events of the twentieth century.

Islam, then, is the dominant faith, and Arabic, Persian, and Turkish are the dominant languages. The older religions and languages of the area have by no means entirely disappeared, and they survive in a mosaic of minorities that make the Middle East a museum of religious and linguistic history. At the time of the Arab conquests, Persia was Zoroastrian, and Egypt and the countries of the Fertile Crescent professed various forms of Christianity. All these countries had important Jewish communities. Of these religions, Zoroastrianism suffered the most. The Persian state, unlike the Christian empire, was completely overcome and destroyed. The Zoroastrians, lacking either the stimulation of powerful friends beyond the border enjoyed by the Christians or the bitter skill in survival possessed by the Jews, fell into discouragement and decline. They took little or no part in the Iranian cultural and political revival in the Middle Ages and are today represented by only a few thousand followers in Iran and a small community in the Indian subcontinent.

Christianity was defeated but not destroyed by the rise of Islam in the Middle East. The processes of settlement, conversion, and assimilation gradually reduced the Christians from a majority to a minority of the population. They retained, however, a vigorous communal and religious life and, secure in the tolerance of the Muslim state, were able to play a minor but significant role in the creation of classical Islamic civilization. The Crusades, with their legacy of conflict and suspicion, brought a permanent worsening in the relations of the Christians with their Muslim neighbors. Although still enjoying the basic rights secured by Muslim law, they were now socially isolated from the Muslims and virtually excluded from the active cultural and political role they had played in the past. The first phases of Westernization and national revival gave the Christian minority, for a while, a new and important function in Middle Eastern life and affairs. The shift from liberal patriotism to communal nationalism and the growth of hostility to the Christian West have again reduced it.

Only in one place did Christians as such continue to play a vital and decisive role. The republic of Lebanon, as formed under the French mandate, was a new creation with new frontiers, but it expressed an old reality. The mountain that formed the core of the so-called Greater Lebanon has since medieval times been a refuge and a citadel of religious and political nonconformity; its people have an old tradition of initiative and independence. In an age of submission, the Lebanese amīrs succeeded, under both Mamluks and Ottomans, in preserving a considerable measure of autonomy. The Christian people of Lebanon, possessing both the Arabic language and a link with the West dating back to the Crusades, were able to make an immense contribution to both the spread of Western culture in the Middle East and the emergence of a new Arab consciousness in response to it. The civil war, which flared up briefly in Lebanon in 1958 and raged from 1975 to 1991, has greatly reduced the role of the Lebanese in Arab affairs and, more important, of the Christians inside Lebanon. Even the city of Beirut, once one of the major commercial, financial, and intellectual centers of the Arab world, has lost its primacy.

The experience of the Jews in the Middle Ages was in general similar to that of the Christians, but diverged sharply in modern times. The Persian Empire had treated them well; the Romans less well, especially in their Judaean homeland, where their repeated attempts to recover their lost independence gave endless trouble to their imperial masters. After the suppression of the last major Jewish revolt against Roman rule in A.D. 135, the Romans made a determined effort to obliterate even the name and memory of Jewish independence. Jerusalem was renamed Aelia, and a temple to Jupiter was erected on the site of the destroyed Jewish Temple. Even the name Judaea was abolished and replaced by Palestina, from the name of the long-vanished Philistines who had once invaded and for a while inhabited the southern coastal strip. After the conversion of Rome to Christianity, the position of the Jews became significantly worse, and in Byzantine times, they became an oppressed minority. The Arab conquest, which found important Jewish communities all over the Middle East, brought a general improvement in their status and security. The main centers of Judaic scholarship and culture had been in Persian Iraq and Byzantine Palestine. Under Muslim rule the Iraqi community flourished, while that of Palestine, now a minor and disturbed border province, fell into a decline. The Jews of Palestine had a particularly difficult time during the Crusades. They were massacred with the Muslims when the Crusaders captured Jerusalem in 1099 and massacred again with the Christians when the Muslims finally reconquered Acre in 1291. Between these two extremes, however, they did manage to maintain some form of Jewish life in Palestine, and in the thirteenth century there were even waves of Jewish immigration from both Muslim North Africa and Christian Europe, including a party of three hundred French and English rabbis who arrived in Jerusalem in 1211. It was not, however, until after the Ottoman conquest at the beginning of the sixteenth century that fresh immigration from other Mediterranean lands led to the establishment of new and vigorous centers of Jewish intellectual activity in Jerusalem and Safed, with far-reaching influence among Jews in other countries, even in Christian Europe.

Like the Christians, the Jews also made an important, though smaller, contribution to classical Islamic civilization. Like them, too, they suffered from the aftermath of the Crusades. The Ottoman conquests and the immigration of the relatively advanced Spanish and Portuguese Jews brought new opportunities, and during the fifteenth and sixteenth centuries they were able to acquire a position of some influence in the Ottoman lands. They lost it during the seventeenth century and were eclipsed, during the eighteenth and nineteenth centuries, by the vigorous and rising eastern Christian communities.

Throughout the period of the dispersion, Jews from other lands had from time to time settled in the Holy Land. Their numbers, however, had been small, and their purposes mainly religious. In the nineteenth century, an entirely new type of immigrant began to come from Eastern and Central Europe, where the spread of nationalist ideologies provided a new ethos for both gentile persecution and Jewish survival. The new immigrants were men and women whose faith was national rather than religious and whose purpose in the Holy Land was not to pray and die but to work and live. The growth of militant anti-Semitism in Europe gave new point and drive to Jewish nationalism. The two European countries with the largest Jewish populations—Czarist Russia and Austria-Hungary—were both, though differently, affected. In Austria-Hungary, anti-Semitism was intellectual and in some degree social. Its effects on the mass of the Jewish population were relatively minor, but its impact on Jewish intellectuals was deeply wounding. It was in the vast and heterogeneous Austro-Hungarian Empire, with its many different nationalities, that Zionism—the idea that there should be a political solution to the Jewish problem, through the restoration of Jewish nationhood and the creation of a Jewish state—was born.

The position of the much larger Jewish communities of the Russian Empire was incomparably worse. Discrimination against Jews was universal and was sanctioned by both law and custom. Persecution was endemic and frequently violent. Caught in an intolerable situation, the Jews found different ways of escape. By far the greatest number solved their problems individually, by emigration above all to America. A small minority sought a political solution by participating in revolutionary movements aimed at the overthrow of the Czarist regime. Another group, also small, chose the Zionist solution of Jewish rebirth and, instead of migrating to the lands of opportunity in the West, chose to migrate to some impoverished and neglected districts of the Ottoman Empire, to which they laid an ancestral claim.

By 1914, there were, according to various estimates, between 60,000 and 85,000 Jews in these districts. In the peace settlement after the First World War, this area was assigned under a mandate by the League of Nations to the British Empire and renamed Palestine. In 1917, by a unilateral declaration, the British government had expressed its approval of the idea of establishing a "Jewish National Home" in Palestine. This principle was incorporated in the text of the mandate, and the mandatary government was empowered to take the necessary steps to ensure its accomplishment, without, however, compromising the rights of the existing population. Not surprisingly, the mandatary power found the combination of these two tasks to be impossible, especially when the rise of Nazism in Germany and the persecution and subsequent destruction of Jewish communities wherever the Nazis held sway sent thousands of Jews from all over continental Europe fleeing for their lives.

The persecuted Jews of Czarist Russia in the late nineteenth and early twentieth centuries had an open world before them. The world depression of the 1930s and the world war and the upheavals in the 1940s offered no such opportunity to refugees and survivors from Nazi Europe. On the contrary, all doors were closed to them. In Western Europe, those who survived the Holocaust were able to reintegrate more or less successfully into their former homelands. No such simple solution was available in Eastern Europe, where the survivors of the Holocaust who endeavored to return to their former homes found themselves confronting old and renewed prejudice, aggravated by a new political order. In the Nazi era and its immediate aftermath, great numbers of Jews from Europe made their way to Palestine, often illegally and despite the efforts of the mandatary authorities, sensitive to Arab hostility, to keep them out.

By 1948, the number of Jews had increased to more than half a million, and when the British government renounced the mandate and the United Nations voted for the creation of Jewish and Arab states in the former mandated territories, the Jews took up their option and proclaimed the state of Israel—the first Jewish state in the Holy Land since the destruction of the ancient Jewish polity by the Roman Empire. An incidental consequence of the establishment of this state was to complete the virtual liquidation—by sometimes voluntary and sometimes forced emigration—of the ancient Jewish communities in the Arab lands, whose position had already been undermined by the new and often intolerant nationalism.

The rise of Jewish nationalism and the emergence of the Jewish state were accompanied by the revival of Hebrew, which had previously survived only as a language of religion, scholarship, and literature and as a medium of communication among learned Jews of different nationalities. In Israel it has become the national language, with Arabic as the second official language. Apart from a few isolated communities of Aramaic-speaking Christian villagers in Syria and in the region around Lake Urmia, the other ancient languages of the Middle East have died out almost completely. In general, the Christian and Jewish minorities in the Arab lands speak Arabic; the Jews of Persia, Persian. The Greek- and Armenian-speaking Christians and Spanish-speaking Jews of Turkey constitute exceptions to the general pattern of linguistic assimilation.

Only one linguistic and ethnic minority of any importance has survived in the central lands of Middle Eastern Islam: the Kurds, who number many millions. The largest Kurdish populations are to be found in Turkey, Iraq, and Iran; there are smaller groups in Syria and Transcaucasia. The Kurdish presence in these lands is well attested throughout the Islamic period, and there is evidence that they have been there since remote antiquity. Although soon converted and deeply committed to Islam, to which Kurdish soldiers, statesmen, and scholars made a significant contribution, they retained their own language and identity. Linguistically, Kurdish is related to Persian; culturally, it is heavily indebted to Arabic, but it remains distinct from both. In medieval times, the Kurds, like the other peoples of the region, defined no national territory and established no national state. There were Islamic dynasties of Kurdish as of other ethnic origins, the most notable of which was that founded by the great Saladin. In an Islamic state, religion, not language or ethnicity, defines political identity, and the Kurds were for the most part content to be Muslims in a Muslim polity. In more recent times, however, the emergence of nationalist ideologies and the attempt to create national states have transformed them into minorities—some of them would say oppressed minorities—in their homelands, and a Kurdish nationalist movement has won increasing support for the argument that the Kurds, like other nations, are entitled to self-determination and national independence, or at least autonomy.

On the fringes of the Middle East zone, a number of other languages remain in use. Afghanistan has two official languages, Pashto and Persian. In North Africa, the indigenous Berber languages are still spoken by very small groups in Libya and Tunisia and by more important minorities in Algeria and Morocco. In all these areas, Berber continues to lose ground to Arabic. In the Caucasian lands, a bewildering variety of languages still flourish. Besides various Turkic and Iranian languages, they include Georgian, Armenian,

Circassian, Chechen, and Avar. According to Pliny, the Romans, in their business dealings with the Caucasian peoples, needed 130 interpreters.[2]

The three main languages of the Middle East show some variation in usage. Persian is the most unified and least extensive. It is the national language of Iran, with comparatively minor dialectal variation within the national frontiers. It is also used in parts of Afghanistan and is very closely related to Tajik, which, however, was in the Soviet era written in the Cyrillic script. Pashto, Kurdish, and some other minor languages belong to the Iranian family, but are distinct from Persian. Arabic, spoken over a vast area from Iraq to Morocco, shows a wide range of spoken dialects, some of them so far apart as to make conversation impossible. But the written language has remained the same, and its unifying power is being reinforced by the spread of education, the press, broadcasting, and the cinema. Turkish is the least unified of the three. At one time, despite a profusion of spoken dialects, the Turkic peoples had only two major literary languages: the Ottoman Turkish of Turkey, and the so-called Chagatay Turkish, which flourished in Central Asia. Both were written in the Arabic script, which, lacking vowels, tended to conceal dialectal variations and made for a wider area of intelligibility. During the nineteenth century, the Turkish of Azerbaijan also became the vehicle of a distinctive literary revival. It was, however, closely related to Ottoman Turkish and much influenced by Ottoman literature. In the twentieth century, the Arabic script has been abolished in almost all Turkish-speaking areas. In Turkey it has been replaced by the Latin script; in the Soviet Union it was first replaced by the Latin script and then, when the Turks had followed suit, by adaptations of the Cyrillic alphabet. The unified Chagatay literary language gave way to a series of "national" languages in the Soviet Middle East, based on spoken dialects and usually not mutually intelligible.

The breakup of the Soviet Union and the independence of the six republics with Muslim majorities brought major changes and a sharp division of opinion as to how this new independence should be exercised. The debate over the alphabets aptly symbolized the alternatives before these peoples. Some chose a return to the Arabic alphabet, which they had used before the Russian Revolution—that is, a return to Islam and, no doubt, closer links with the Islamic states of the region and especially with their nearest neighbor, Iran. Some preferred to retain the Cyrillic script and remain part of a looser, more open association of former Soviet states. Still others, especially in Azerbaijan, opted for the Turkish Latin script—that is, the secular, modernizing, and democratic way of life, already taken by the people of the Turkish Republic. It is a choice, one might say, between Kemalism, Khomeinism, and post-Sovietism.

We have now defined the "Middle East" in terms of geography and history, of religion, language, and culture. It may be useful to attempt a closer definition in terms of present-day political entities. Obviously, one cannot demarcate the frontiers of a zone or region, as one would of a state or province. Except on the seacoasts, the Middle East tapers off in an indeterminate borderland of countries that have much in common with it, yet are not wholly part of it. In current usage, the Middle East consists of Turkey, Iran, and perhaps Afghanistan; of Iraq and the Arabian peninsula; of the four Levant states of Syria, Lebanon, Israel, and Jordan; and of Egypt, with variously defined extensions southward and westward into Arabic-speaking Africa. The southern limit of the Middle East is set in Asia by the seas that wash the shores of Iran and the Arabian peninsula, in Africa, by that vague and contested borderland where Arab and black Africa meet, often in regions of endemic conflict, like the Sudan, Chad, and Mauritania. The one clearly defined limit of the Middle East in current usage has been in the north, where it was usually identified with the Soviet frontier. But this was always historically and culturally inaccurate and no longer corresponds to currently evolving realities. North of the Soviet–Turkish, Soviet–Iranian, and Soviet–Afghan frontiers in Transcaucasia, the Caucasus, and Central Asia are countries that until the nineteenth century were still an integral part of the Middle Eastern world. In earlier days, they belonged to the great Arab, Persian, and Turkic empires of Islam, of which such great Muslim cities as Samarkand and Bukhara were as essential a part as Baghdad or Cairo, Isfahan or Istanbul. Georgia and Armenia are Christian countries on the edge of the Middle East; they have, however, at times been of some importance in Middle Eastern affairs, and many of their peoples have played a variety of roles in the Islamic lands. Of the other southern and Central Asian republics, five are inhabited by Turkic-speaking and, the sixth by Iranian-speaking, Muslims, closely akin in their religious, cultural, and political traditions to the lands of what we have conventionally called the Middle East. After the liquidation of the last British footholds in the Persian Gulf in 1971, these Soviet republics were indeed the only parts of the Middle East that were still incorporated in a non–Middle Eastern political system with its capital in Europe. This anomaly, too, has ended.

Until the Iranian revolution in 1979, it might have seemed that too much stress had been laid on Islam—on religion—in defining the Middle East, which is, after all, a twentieth-century term and which consists of a group of nationally defined states professing strong nationalist and/or patriotic sentiments. There was a time not so long ago when the stamp of Islam in the Middle East seemed to be growing dim. But it was by no means effaced, and it is now clearer than ever.

Religion means different things to different people. In the West it means principally a system of belief and worship, distinct from, and in modern times usually subordinate to, national and political allegiances. But for Muslims it conveys a great deal more than that. Islam is a civilization, a term that corresponds to Christendom as well as Christianity in the West. No doubt, many local, national, and regional traditions and characteristics have survived among the Muslim peoples and have gained greatly in importance in modern times, but on all the peoples that have accepted them, the faith and law of Islam have impressed a stamp of common identity, which remains even when faith is lost and the law has been abandoned.

This common identity rests, in the first instance, on the Muslim creed that "God is One and Muḥammad is His Prophet," on the Qur'ān and the traditions, and on the whole subtle and complex system of theology and law that has evolved from them. The teachings of historical Islam, besides moral and ritual precepts and theological dogmas, include much that in the West would be called law: civil, criminal, and even constitutional law. For the traditional Muslim believer, these laws emanate from the same source and possess the same authority as do the laws of conduct and worship. The political traditions of the Islamic peoples were shaped for centuries by the formulations of the doctors of the holy law and by the memories of the Muslim empires of the past. Their languages, irrespective of origin, were written in the same Arabic script and borrowed an immense vocabulary of Arabic words, especially of terms belonging to two closely related fields of endeavor, one of religion and culture and the other of law and government.

It is not difficult to recognize an Islamic work of art. Anyone, even with a limited knowledge of art and architecture, can look through a folder of photographs of buildings and objects and pick out those that are Islamic. The arcade and minaret of the mosque, the arabesque and geometrical patterns of decoration, the rules of sequence and association of both poetry and cookery—all these, despite many variations, show a fundamental unity of tradition and aesthetic that is Islamic, and derives essentially from Middle Eastern—Arabic, Persian, or Turkish—archetypes. In music, buildings, carpets, and cuisine, this unity in diversity of Islamic civilization can be heard, touched, seen, and tasted. It is also present, though less easy to identify and understand, in such things as law, government, and institutions, in social and political attitudes and ideas.

The Islamic history of the Middle East was begun by the great Arab conquests of the seventh and eighth centuries, which, for the first time since Alexander, created a united imperial system from North Africa to the borders of India and China. The territorial and administrative unity of the Arab Empire was in time eroded and destroyed by invasion, dissension, and the processes of political fragmentation; the dominance of the Arab nation was challenged and ended by the rise of other nations within Islam. But the religious and cultural unity of Middle Eastern Islam survived, and was symbolized in the ideal unity of the caliphate, which all agreed to respect. There were moments of grave danger when Islam was threatened from both east and west, but they were overcome. The Turks indeed came as conquerors, but they were converted and assimilated and brought new strength and vigor to a faltering society and polity. With that strength, Islam was able to hold and repel another invasion, that of the Crusaders, from the west.

From both directions, however, new and deadlier blows were to follow. On two occasions, the Islamic Middle East was crushed and overwhelmed by alien invaders who dominated it by force of arms and, if they did not destroy the old civilization, sapped the confidence of those who maintained it and turned them on to new paths. The first was the invasion of the heathen Mongols from eastern Asia, who ended the Baghdad caliphate and, for the first time since the Prophet, subjected some of the heartlands of Islam to non-Islamic rule. The second was the impact of the modern West.

2

~~~~~~~~~~

The Impact of the West

It has been our practice for some time now to speak of the group of countries to which we belong as the West, a term that is no longer a purely geographical expression, but also denotes a cultural, social, and, until recently, a political and military entity. What are the geographical boundaries of this entity—not merely of the Western alliance, which are fairly obvious, but of the larger entity whose will to survive the alliance expressed? The westernmost limit of the West is clear enough: the Pacific coast—and dependencies—of North America. The eastern limit is more problematic. Leaving aside the local American concept of the West, the West as a cultural or civilizational entity has generally been understood to cover both shores of the North Atlantic and to extend into Europe to a point that has been variously fixed, at various times and for various purposes, on the Channel, the Rhine, the Elbe, the Oder, the Vistula, the Bosphorus, and the Ural Mountains, the conventional boundary between Europe and Asia.

The West is most easily defined in relation to the East, and of course there is more than one East. In the West, when we used to speak of East–West contrasts and conflicts, we usually meant the Cold War and its ramifications. In this sense, the East meant the Soviet or Communist blocs (the two were not identical); the West meant the Western alliance and its associates, sometimes loosely called the free world. It included, in this context, a string of more or less dictatorial regimes on several continents, but excluded Sweden, Switzerland, Ireland, and, of course, Finland.

The former Soviet East is not, however, our only point of reference. There is also what one might call, with only apparent tautology, the Oriental East—the many countries, societies, and peoples of Asia and, for that matter, of Africa who, however they may differ among themselves, have this much in common; that the Christian or post-Christian civilization of Europe and its daughters is alien to them, that they have for long been subject to its domination or influence, and that they have now brought that subjection to an end. For many in the Middle East and also, to a diminishing extent, in other parts of Asia, the real East–West struggle is and has long been this, and its purpose is to remove the last vestiges of Western imperial domination in the East. The Western–Soviet conflict, according to this view, was an irrelevance: useful in many ways, no doubt, but not directly of concern to the Eastern peoples. One might even argue that Russia itself is really a part of the West, with which it was linked by its dominant European population, its Judeo-Christian and Greco-Roman background, its scientific and industrial development, and, some would add, its predatory habits. Recent developments in the former Soviet Union clearly indicate a growing desire by the Russians to reclaim and reassert their Western, or, to be more precise, their European, heritage.

In the Middle East, the term "West," expressing a cultural and political entity, is a comparatively new one, almost as new as the term "Middle East" and, like it, of Western origin. But again, like the term "Middle East," it denotes an ancient reality long known and familiar under other names. In recent years, some attention has been given to the problem of national images and stereotypes, and some writers have sought to describe and classify the memories and prejudices that shape Western attitudes toward the Middle East and their influence on the formation of Western policy. Far less attention has been given to the origins and development of Middle Eastern attitudes toward the West, though these are of at least equal importance in determining relations between the two. In the absence of the rather Western habits of self-analysis and self-criticism, they may even be of greater importance.

The word "West" has been used since medieval times by Muslim writers, but not to denote Christian Europe. Islam had its own west, in North Africa and Spain, reaching as far as the Atlantic, and had no reason to apply this term to the infidel and barbarian lands that lay to the north of the Mediterranean Sea. For the medieval

Muslim, the world was divided into two great zones, the house of Islam and the house of war. South and east of the house of Islam, the house of war was inhabited by pagans and idolaters, ready for conquest and ripe for conversion. North and northwest lay the empires and kingdoms of Christendom, the greatest rival of the Islamic faith, the deadliest enemy of Islamic power. At first it was the Greek Christians of Byzantium who sustained the shocks of Islamic attack; later, while Byzantium faltered and finally succumbed to Turkish conquest, the Franks of western Europe counterattacked from Spain to Palestine, in Africa and in Asia. From late medieval times onward, the image of the European Christian changed in Muslim minds. The Orthodox Greek, now a fellow subject of the Turkish sultan, ceased to be a redoubtable foe and became a harmless neighbor. His place as enemy in chief was taken by the Frank. This term, commonly applied to the Crusaders in contemporary Arabic writings, was generalized to cover the Catholic—later also Protestant—peoples of central and western Europe, to distinguish them from the Muslims, on the one hand, and the Greek Orthodox Christians, on the other.

For the medieval Muslim, the Franks were a race of barbarous infidels, of little interest or concern to the peoples of Islam. In the Muslim worldview, Christianity, like Judaism, was in origin a true faith, representing an earlier link in the chain of divine revelations that had culminated in the final and perfect revelation vouchsafed to Muḥammad. What was true in it was preserved in Islam; the rest was accretion and distortion. Christianity, and with it the Christian civilization founded on it, could accordingly be dismissed as something incomplete, superseded, and debased. This view is certainly more tolerant than that of contemporary Christian Europe, which regarded Islam as something subsequent to God's final revelation and therefore wholly false and evil, and it is reflected in the far greater tolerance accorded to the followers of the rival faith. This, however, did not make for any greater esteem. The Greeks were custodians of an ancient civilization from whom something could be learned and with whom a form of coexistence had been evolved in the course of the centuries. The wild, fierce tribes of darkest Europe were thought to have no such redeeming features. It is noteworthy that while many works were translated into Arabic from Greek, Syriac, old Persian, and other languages, only one book—a late Roman history—was translated from Latin and none from any other Western language throughout the Middle Ages.

This attitude may have been justified in the so-called Dark Ages, when Frankish Europe really was backward and inferior; it can only have been reinforced by the conduct of the Crusaders in the Middle East and elsewhere. But already in the high Middle Ages it was becoming dangerously out of date.

From the end of the fifteenth century, the peoples of Europe embarked on a vast movement of expansion—commercial, political, cultural, and demographic—which by the twentieth century had brought almost the whole world into the orbit of European civilization. It was an expansion at both ends; while the Portuguese and Spaniards, the English, Dutch, and French sailed across the oceans from western Europe to discover new worlds and conquer old ones, the Russians advanced southward and eastward across the steppes, toward the Middle East and into Asia.

At both ends of Europe this expansion began with a reconquest, developing along similar and almost contemporary lines. In the East, the rulers of Muscovy, after a long struggle, liberated their city and land from the rule of the Muslim Tatars, whose final attack they defeated in 1480. In the West, the Portuguese and then the Spaniards completed the reconquest of the Iberian peninsula from the Arabs and Moors, who had invaded it eight centuries previously, and won their final victory with the capture of Granada, the last Muslim state in western Europe, in 1492. At both ends of Europe, the victorious Christians followed their former masters whence they had come— the Russians into Tartary and Asia, the Iberians into Africa and beyond. There were, of course, obvious military reasons for pursuing the attack: to complete the destruction of the enemy, giving him no time to regroup and mount a counterattack. But soon the reconquest became a conquest, sustained by the same momentum and inspired by the same mixture of religious and material motives.

This process of expansion has gone through various forms and phases and has been known by various names. One of them is colonization; others are the white man's burden, manifest destiny, and whatever synonym the Russians may use for the process that carried them from Muscovy to the Urals and from the Urals to the Pacific. In some areas, the process of colonization was so successful and so complete that the previous inhabitants were displaced or reduced to insignificance, and the colonizers were strong enough to stand on their own feet without needing to lean any longer on the mother country. The French in North Africa did not quite reach this point; the English in North America did. In most of Asia and Africa, the original cultures and peoples were too strong and too deeply rooted to be displaced, and the colonizers were limited to the role of overlords and rulers. The result was the classic imperial system of government as it existed in the nineteenth and early twentieth centuries.

In the Middle East, the impact of European imperialism was late, brief, and, for the most part, indirect. The impact of Europe was, however, profound and overwhelming.

At first, this impact was entirely economic. Both politically and militarily, the European states were far weaker than the Islamic states of the Middle East, and they came not as masters or rulers, still less as invaders, but as humble petitioners seeking the grace and favor of the lords of Islam and asking only permission to buy and sell in the seaports and in a few towns in the interior. The first European footholds in the Mediterranean Islamic seaports had been gained during the Crusades. They remained even after the defeat and expulsion of the Crusaders, and in Ottoman times they grew, expanded, and flourished.

In the trade between the maritime states of Western Europe and the Muslim states of the Middle East, the Westerners had several practical advantages. Their ships, built to face the Atlantic gales, were stronger, larger, and more maneuverable than those of the Muslim powers. They could carry more guns and also larger cargoes, and they could travel greater distances at relatively low cost. Once they had explored the eastern seas, they were able to bring goods from South and Southeast Asia to the Middle East; once they had consolidated their tropical and semitropical colonies in the Americas and Southeast Asia, they were able to supply a much wider range of merchandise than in medieval times.

Perhaps more important than this was a different attitude toward production and commerce. The rise of mercantilism in the producer-oriented West helped European trading companies and the states that protected and encouraged them to achieve a level of commercial organization and a concentration of economic energies unknown and unparalleled in the consumer-oriented Islamic Middle East, where—as a matter of fact more than theory—"market forces" operated without serious restriction. The Western trading corporations, with the help of their business-minded governments, represented an entirely new force. Their power was enormously increased when Western Europeans were installed in South and Southeast Asia not only as traders, but also as rulers, and they were therefore able to control the trade in spices and other commodities between Asia and Europe from both ends. Western merchants, and later manufacturers and eventually governments, were able to establish almost total domination of Middle Eastern markets and ultimately even of many major Middle Eastern manufactures.

It is easy to cite examples. Middle Eastern textiles, once highly regarded in the West, were driven first from external and then even from domestic markets by Western goods, which, though certainly not better, were more efficiently and cheaply produced and more aggressively marketed. Even coffee and sugar, two items that once figured prominently among Middle Eastern exports to the West, where they were previously unknown, were in time produced by the Western powers in their tropical colonies, and eventually—thanks again to cheaper production and better marketing—they were transferred from the export to the import side of Middle Eastern trade with Western Europe. By the eighteenth century, when a Turk or an Arab indulged in a cup of sweetened coffee, in all probability the coffee had been brought by Dutch merchants from Java and the sugar by British or French merchants from the West Indies. Only the hot water was of local provenance. In the course of the nineteenth century, even that became doubtful, as Western companies dominated the rapidly expanding utilities in Middle Eastern cities.

In the early days of European expansion, in the late fifteenth and early sixteenth centuries, it might well have seemed that the Middle East was about to be caught between the two pincers of the west Europeans, advancing by sea from the southeast, from their bases in India, and the Russians coming down from the north. But that danger in its military and political form was averted. A new power had arisen in the Middle East, able to hold both the Black and Red seas for Islam and to halt the northern and the southern intruders. The beginnings of European expansion had coincided with the emergence of two new Middle Eastern empires: the Safavid state in Iran and the Ottoman state in Turkey. In the early years of the sixteenth century, a bitter struggle between the two for supremacy in the Middle East resulted in an Ottoman victory. The Arab lands, already long accustomed to the rule of Turkish and other alien military castes, became part of the Ottoman Empire for four hundred years.

Shielded by the military might of the Ottoman Empire from invasion and by the panoply of traditional learning from reality, the peoples of the Middle East continued to cherish the ancient human myth of self-sufficiency—to believe, as other societies before and after them have believed, in the immeasurable and immutable superiority of their own way of life and to despise the barbarous Western infidel from an altitude of correct doctrine reinforced by military power.

The succession of Ottoman victories over Christian adversaries during the sixteenth century can only have encouraged this attitude; the military stalemate of the seventeenth century brought no real reason to modify it. The real change began only when the Ottoman Empire suffered decisive and unmistakable defeats: defeats in battle followed by loss of territory and peace treaties dictated by victorious enemies. It was a new and painful experience and initiated a long and difficult adjustment that has not yet been completed.

The process began with the second Turkish siege of Vienna, in 1683. The Turkish failure this time was decisive and final, and was followed by a rapid advance of the Austrians and their allies deep into Ottoman territory. In 1696 the Russians seized Azov, thus gaining their first foothold on the Black Sea; in 1699 the Austrians imposed the treaty of Carlowitz—the first to be signed by the Ottoman Empire as a defeated power. Despite occasional rallies, the processes of defeat, humiliation, and withdrawal continued during the eighteenth century, the bitterest blow of all being the Russian annexation, in 1783, of the old Turkish, Islamic land of the Crimea.

The problem first appeared as military, and the first remedies propounded were also military. The Ottoman armies had been defeated in the field by European armies; it might therefore be wise to adopt European weapons, training, and techniques. From time to time during the eighteenth century, military instructors were imported from Europe, technical schools were established, and Turkish officers and cadets were instructed in the European arts of war. It was a small beginning, but an immensely significant one. For the first time, young Muslims, instead of despising the uncouth Westerners, were accepting them as guides and teachers, learning their languages, and reading their books. By the end of the eighteenth century, the young artillery cadet who had learned French to read his gunnery manual could find other reading matter, more explosive and more penetrating.

The military reforms, though the first and for long the most important, were not the only breaches in the wall of self-sufficiency. In 1729 the first Turkish printing press was established in Istanbul; by 1742, when it was closed, it had printed seventeen books, including a description of France by a Turkish ambassador sent there in 1721 and a treatise on the military arts as applied in the armies of Europe. The loss of cultural self-confidence can also be seen in the European influences that began to affect Ottoman architecture, even religious architecture, as in the Italianate baroque ornamentation of the Nuruosmaniye mosque, completed in 1755.

The feeling of weakness and decline induced by military defeat must have been reinforced by the rapid increase in European exports to the Middle East, now extending beyond luxury products to include such staples as sugar and coffee. It was a time of discouragement that variously found expression in a withdrawal of consent from Ottoman supremacy, in a first, tentative groping toward European ways, in the currency of an Islamic saying, now repeated with a new meaning and a new poignancy: "This world is the prison of the believers and the paradise of the unbelievers."[1]

During the eighteenth century, the chief territorial threat to the Middle East came from the north, where the military empire of Russia advanced steadily toward the Black Sea and the Caucasus. England and France—by now Asian as well as European powers—were the chief commercial rivals, competing in the markets of Egypt, the Levant, and Persia.

The invasion of Egypt by a French expeditionary force under General Napoleon Bonaparte in 1798 opened a new phase in the history of Western impact. Both Western and Middle Eastern historians have seen it as a watershed in history: the first armed inroad of the modern West into the Middle East, the first shock to Islamic complacency, the first impulse to Westernization and reform. In all these respects, it was to some extent anticipated by the Turkish defeats in the north and by the Turkish response to them. Its importance, however, remains considerable. To the Muslims, Bonaparte demonstrated how easily a modern European army could invade, conquer, and govern one of the heartlands of Islam; to the British, how easily a hostile power could cut their overland route to India. Both parties, in their different ways, learned the lesson, drew inferences, and took action. The French expedition brought the problems of impact and response, in an acute form, to the Arab lands; it also inaugurated a century and a half of direct Anglo-French involvement in the affairs of these lands.

The menace from the north had by no means ended. By the eighteenth century, the Russians had won control of the northern and eastern shores of the Black Sea, now no longer a Muslim lake. In 1800 they annexed Georgia; in 1806 they captured Baku; and in the early decades of the nineteenth century they took from Persia and from local rulers the provinces now forming the former Soviet republics of Armenia and Azerbaijan.

The 1850s and 1860s were a period of rapid and significant development in the Middle East. The Crimean War had the usual catalytic effect of a major war, bringing swift and sudden changes and a new intensity of feeling and experience. The alliance with Britain and France and the arrival of British and French troops in Turkey brought contacts with the West on a scale without precedent.

Halted in the nearer east by the Crimean War, the Russians turned their attention to Central Asia, where in the 1860s and 1870s they subjugated the khanates of Khokand, Bukhara, and Khiva. The annexation of the area between the Caspian Sea and the Oxus River in the 1880s consolidated their position in Central Asia and on the northeastern frontier of Persia. A different kind of problem arose in Ottoman Europe, where the rise of nationalist movements threatened the Turks with both the loss of territory and the contamination of dangerous ideas.

In the Arab lands, the interference and influence of the West passed through several phases. In the first half of the nineteenth century, the Western interest was chiefly in trade and transit. True, there was some territorial encroachment, as in the Persian Gulf and in southern Arabia, where the British seized Aden in 1839, but these advances were limited to the far periphery and were concerned primarily with the security of the sea-lanes. The interests of Great Britain, by now the most active Western power in the Middle East, were served by the famous policy of "maintaining the integrity and independence of the Ottoman Empire." It seemed reasonable to assume that the Turks, as the dominant and established power in the area, would align themselves with those whose interests were purely economic and strategic, against a potential enemy whose aims were expansionist and disruptive. This British policy was abandoned only with extreme reluctance and with many nostalgic hankerings. In a sense, first British and then American policies in the Middle East in recent years have represented a series of inconclusive attempts to discover or, failing that, to create a Middle Eastern power whose integrity and independence they could maintain and whose rulers, in return, would safeguard their vital interests. It may be noted that both the British and the Ottomans were rather better at this game of protection than were any subsequent players of the roles of protector and protégé.

The second half of the nineteenth century brought important changes. The rapid modernization of the transit routes, the growth of direct Western economic and financial interest in the area, and, from the 1880s onward, the extension of German influence in Turkey led to a realignment of British policy. The occupation of Egypt, undertaken in 1882 for a limited purpose and a limited time, became permanent and was extended to the Sudan. In 1918 the Ottoman

Empire, which for four centuries had held the Arab lands, was defeated and destroyed, and a series of new, unfamiliar political structures were assembled from the debris.

Between 1918 and 1945, Britain and France, in fitful association and rivalry, were the dominant powers in the Arab East. Aden, Palestine, and the Sudan were ruled directly through regimes of a colonial type; elsewhere, control—if that is the right word—was indirect. It was maintained through local governments, some of them under mandate, others nominally independent, with a variable and uncertain degree of responsibility for their own affairs. These arrangements ended in the years following the Second World War, when all the countries of the Arab Middle East acquired full political independence and found new leaders and guides to exercise it on their behalf.

The century and a half of Anglo-French preeminence in the Middle East—from the mighty conflict of Nelson and Napoleon to the futile collaboration of Eden and Mollet in the failed Suez expedition of 1956—and the somewhat longer period of Westernizing influences in Turkey brought immense and irreversible changes on every level of social existence. By no means were all the changes the work of Western rulers and overlords, most of whom tended to be cautiously conservative in their policies. Some of the most crucial changes were due to vigorous and ruthless Middle Eastern Westernizers—rulers who sought to acquire and master the Western instruments of power, merchants anxious to use Western techniques to amass wealth, men of letters and of action fascinated by the potency of Western knowledge and ideas. The processes of change are symbolically reflected in the progressive adoption of Western dress. Only once before in history had the Muslims departed from their own customs and adopted a foreign style of dress; that was when the Mamluk amīrs of late-thirteenth-century Egypt, by order of the sultan, wore Mongol robes and accoutrements and let their hair grow in the Mongol manner. The same kind of sympathetic magic no doubt inspired the adoption of trousers, tunics, and frockcoats in the nineteenth century—first in the army, by order; then in the civil service, again by order; finally among the nonofficial urban literate classes, by a kind of social osmosis. The Mongol style was abandoned at the beginning of the fourteenth century, perhaps because the Mongols themselves were becoming Muslims. The coats and pants of Europe, however, still remain and have become the outward sign and symbol of literacy and modernity. In our own day, the last bastion of Muslim conservatism is falling, as the turban and the tarbush disappear, and the brimmed, peaked, and vizored headgear of the West replaces them. The soldiers of Islamic revolutionary Iran still wear Western-style uniforms. Even the diplomats of the Islamic republic—unlike those of the monarchs of Arabia—still wear Western clothes, with only the omission of the necktie to symbolize their rejection of Western ways and constraints.

The beginning was purely military: the simple desire for survival in a world dominated by an expanding and advancing Europe. This required armies in the European style—a simple matter, so it seemed, of training and equipment, to be solved by borrowing a few instructors and indenting for the appropriate supplies. Yet the task of running the new-style armies led inescapably to the building of schools to officer them and the reform of education, to the formation of departments to maintain them and the reform of government, to the creation and administration by the state of services and factories to supply them, and, very tardily, to the reform of the economy.

Economic and technological progress was for a long time largely the work of Europeans. It was they who built roads, railways, bridges, and ports; brought the steam engine in the nineteenth and the petrol engine in the twentieth century, gas and electricity, telegraphy and radio, and the first beginnings of industrial development. Sometimes they came in their own interest as servants of their governments or of concessionary companies, sometimes as experts or advisers employed by Middle Eastern governments and by other entrepreneurs. At first they employed only unskilled local labor, then also semiskilled artisans; finally they were able to draw on important local reserves of technical and professional skill, of the men who ultimately took over from them.

Surely the most important foreign enterprise in the twentieth century was the discovery and exploitation of oil, which placed enormous revenues at the disposal of those Middle Eastern governments that ruled over the lands in which the oil was found. Already in medieval times, Muslim armies had admired and appreciated European weapons, and European merchants were never lacking to provide them for a price. In a letter to the caliph in Baghdad, Saladin explained how European merchants, by supplying him with their most up-to-date weaponry, were contributing to their own defeat and destruction. Some centuries later, European shipwrights, gun founders, and other makers of weapons of war contributed to the Ottoman advance into the heart of Europe. The enormous wealth accruing from the sale of oil enabled Middle Eastern governments to acquire the most modern and the most deadly creations of the Western armaments industry and—as Saddam Hussein demonstrated—to use them as they chose. In buying Western weapons to fight the West, he was following a tradition that was centuries old. So, too, were those who sold them to him.

With European weapons and technology came another importation, European ideas, which were to prove at least equally disruptive to the old social and political order. Until the eighteenth century, the world of Islam had been cut off from almost all intellectual and cultural contact with the West. The Renaissance and the new learning, the scientific, technological, and intellectual movements of Christian Europe found no echo and awoke no response among peoples to whom they were profoundly alien and utterly irrelevant. Even the impact of European commerce and diplomacy, though it could not be wholly avoided, was cushioned and absorbed by an intermediate class of native Christians and, to a lesser extent, Jews who, as merchants, agents, go-betweens, and interpreters, protected their Muslim masters from the contamination of direct contact. The Ottoman Empire in the days of its greatness maintained no resident embassies abroad. Even its dealings with the foreign embassies in Istanbul passed through the hands of the Grand Dragoman, who was usually a Greek. There were very few Muslims with a reading knowledge of a Western language; with a few, trifling exceptions, there were no Arabic, Persian, or Turkish translations of Western books. In the words of an Ottoman historian, "Familiar association with heathens and infidels is forbidden to the people of Islam, and friendly and intimate intercourse between two parties that are to one another as darkness and light is far from desirable."[2]

The military reform changed all that. Instead of an ignorant barbarian, the Frank became a teacher of the noblest and most crucial of arts, that of war. His language was no longer an "uncouth jargon," as one writer had called it, but the key to essential knowledge.

The military reformers had intended to open a sluice gate in the wall, with a limited and regulated flow. Instead they admitted a flood, a foaming, frothing flood that came seeping and bursting through a thousand cracks, bringing destruction and the seeds of new life. It was a flood that seemed to have no end, as the apparently inexhaustible inventiveness of Europe produced more and newer ideas for each generation to master. During the nineteenth century, two trends predominated, sometimes in harmony, often in conflict with each other: the radical liberalism of the French Revolution and the authoritarian reformism of the Enlightenment.

There were many new channels through which Western ideas could percolate and penetrate to the hitherto sealed world of Islam. Such, for example, were the Muslim visitors from the Middle East, who now began to appear in increasing numbers in the capitals of Europe. Some few intrepid travelers had ventured, even in earlier times, to brave the dangers of unknown Europe, but from the Crusades to the seventeenth century barely a score left any written record—almost all of them official envoys on special missions. In 1791 the Ottoman sultan Selim III sent Ebubekir Ratib Efendi to Vienna, where he produced a detailed report on enlightened despotism at work, with recommendations for reform in the Ottoman Empire. In the succeeding years, the sultan established the first resident embassies in London, Vienna, Berlin, and Paris. They were followed by Persian embassies in the nineteenth century and, informally, by representatives of the new independent power that had arisen in Egypt under Muḥammad ʿAlī and his successors. At a time when a knowledge of foreign languages and an acquaintance with foreign countries were rare and vital qualifications, these embassies provided unique opportunities for acquiring them, and the men who had served in them formed an important element in the new political elite. Neither the ulema nor the army but the translation chambers and the embassies were now the high road to influence and power.

After the diplomats, the second—and in the long run more important—group of Middle Easterners to appear in Europe were the students. The first Egyptian student mission was sent to Italy by Muḥammad ʿAlī Pasha in 1809, and by 1818 there were 23 Egyptian students in Europe. The first Persian student mission appeared in England at about the same time. In 1826 the pasha of Egypt sent the first large Egyptian mission, of 44 students, to Paris. What the pasha could do, the sultan could do better, and in 1827 Sultan Mahmud II, despite strong religious opposition, sent an Ottoman mission of about 150 students to various countries. Over the years hundreds of others followed them, the forerunners of the countless thousands that were still to come. It is a well-known fact that students learn more from one another than from their teachers, and in the universities of Europe in the 1820s, 1830s, and 1840s, there was much to learn.

It was no doubt in part because of this instruction that during the 1860s, a third wave of visitors appeared—exiles. The Young

Ottomans were a group of more or less liberal patriots who found it expedient to leave Turkey and continue their criticisms of the sultan's ministers from Europe, where they published opposition journals in London, Paris, and Geneva and had them smuggled into Turkey. They were followed in the late nineteenth century and early twentieth century by other liberal and patriotic groups, collectively and rather loosely known as the Young Turks. From time to time, other groups of political exiles came from the Middle East, but on the whole they have been surprisingly few and inactive.

Besides Middle Eastern visitors to the West, there were Western visitors to the Middle East: teachers and scholars, experts and advisers, missionaries and propagandists, as well as political and commercial entrepreneurs of many kinds. The first to exercise personal influence over young Muslims were the European military instructors employed in Turkey, Egypt, and later Persia. Most of them were French, and the language they used was naturally French. The revolution in France did not break this link, and as late as 1796 the imperial Ottoman government sent a request to the Committee of Public Safety in Paris to supply a number of military experts and technicians. They came under the orders of the new French ambassador, General Aubert Dubayet, a native of New Orleans and a fervent revolutionary who had fought in America under Lafayette. The military school in Istanbul, we are told, had a library of four hundred books, many of them French, including a set of the *Grande Encyclopédie.* Every university teacher knows that the presence of books in an academic library does not prove that anyone reads them, particularly when the books are in a foreign language and express unfamiliar ideas. All we can say is that the books were accessible and that some of the ideas appear in later generations. Muḥammad ʿAlī in Egypt also recruited French officers, of whom many were available after 1815. His school of mathematics in Cairo had a library with French books, including works by Rousseau and Voltaire and books on European institutions. Many other military missions followed, from a variety of countries, among them a first group of American officers who went to Egypt after the Civil War. Of all groups in Middle Eastern society, the army officers have had the longest and most intensive exposure to Western influence and have the most vital professional interest in modernization and reform. This may help explain the Middle Eastern phenomenon, unusual in other parts of the world, of the professional officer as the spearhead of social change.

Although the officer-instructors were the first Western teachers, there were many others—teachers of every subject in every kind of school. Some taught in the modern-style schools and colleges that were being set up, in increasing numbers, by Middle Eastern governments; others in schools created by foreign missions and governments as a service to humanity and an instrument of cultural policy. They were joined in both groups by growing numbers of Westernized Middle Easterners who had studied in Western schools at home or abroad and had mastered a Western language and skill.

Between 1854 and 1856, the lessons of war came in a new form and with a new intensity. The Crimean War was far from being the first fought by Turkey against Russia, nor was it the first occasion when Turkey had the support of European Christian allies. But in the past, these had been remote and barely visible—cobelligerents against a common enemy rather than allies in any true sense. This time, Britain and France were allies and comrades in arms, with armies on Turkish soil and fleets in Turkish waters engaged in a common war effort. This led to rapid and extensive contacts between Turks and West Europeans at many levels. The large Western presence in Turkish cities—civilian and technical as well as military—inaugurated many important changes. Some were positive—for example, the extension of the telegraph to Istanbul. The arrival for the first time of correspondents working for daily papers set an example and in time provided an opportunity for the new Turkish newspapers. The foreign presence also gave a new impetus to the improvement of street lighting, transport, and other amenities.

Some of the changes were more equivocal. As an ally of Britain and France, the sultan was enabled to raise war loans in Western financial markets and thus enter the slippery slope to extravagance and bankruptcy.

The dissemination of Western knowledge and ideas was enormously helped by the spread, in various forms, of the European book. As a knowledge of European languages became more common, European books found readers and, more important, translators. During the sixteenth century, two books of Western origin are known to have appeared in Turkish; one—never printed—was a history of France, translated in 1572 by order of the Reis Efendi, the chief secretary in charge of foreign affairs; and the other was an account of the discovery and wonders of the New World, compiled from European sources in about 1580. The seventeenth century brought a couple of books on history and geography and a treatise on the diagnosis and treatment of syphilis, which the Turks, and after them, other Middle Eastern peoples, call *firengi*; the eighteenth added a few more, including some translations of French books on the military sciences that were printed in Istanbul. Until the end of the eighteenth century, there were still only a handful of Western works available in Turkish, most of them dry and factual compilations prepared for official use; there were none at all in Arabic or Persian.

The first impulse to the new translation movement seems to have come from the French, for frankly propagandist purposes. Thus, for example, the address of the National Convention to the French people, of 9 October 1794, was translated into Arabic and published in a quarto booklet with the French and Arabic texts on facing pages, a useful aid to students of language and of other things. Other French political writings were translated into Arabic and Turkish and distributed in the Middle East. The French expedition to Egypt made detailed arrangements for the publication of French news and opinion in Arabic.

The immediate impact of all this was, as far as we know, limited. Far more influential was the translation movement that developed during the nineteenth century in the three main centers, in Turkey, Egypt, and Persia. At first it was all officially sponsored and reveals a rather official trend of thought. The first translations made and published under the auspices of Middle Eastern rulers include works on Napoleon and Catherine of Russia, Voltaire's *Peter the Great* and *Charles XII*, Robertson's *Charles V*, and the instructions of Frederick the Great to his commanders. Later the work was taken up and immensely developed by the enterprise of editors, publishers, printers, and translators.

The West had offered new media of communication—printing in the eighteenth, journalism and the telegraph in the nineteenth, and radio and television in the twentieth century—all of which played a great role in the dissemination of Western and other ideas. The first newspapers were mainly official; for example, the leading article in the first issue of the Ottoman official gazette, published on 14 May 1832, defines the function of the press as being to make known the true nature of events and the real purpose of the acts and commands of the government, in order to prevent misunderstanding and forestall uninformed criticism; another purpose was to provide useful knowledge on commerce, science, and the arts. The first nonofficial newspaper in Turkish was a weekly founded in 1840 by an Englishman called William Churchill. It was followed by many others, in Turkish, Arabic, and Persian, as well as other languages.

With the press came the journalist, a new and portentous figure in Middle Eastern life. Another newcomer, no less important, was the lawyer. In the old days, law was holy law, a branch of religious learning, and the only lawyers were the ulema. Legal and constitutional reform, the creation of modern laws and of courts to administer them, brought into existence a new class of secular advocates, who played a great role in the new political life and in the application of new political ideas and methods.

The journalists and lawyers, like the new-style officers and officials, required a new type of education in place of the traditional religious and literary learning of the past. Their pabulum was Western languages and literature, history, geography, and law, to which were later added economics and politics. Most of these subjects were new and strange; they were, however, familiar in that they were all literary in form, capable of being learned from books or lectures and then memorized. They could thus be assimilated into traditional methods of education, relying chiefly on the authority of the teacher and the memory of the student.

The practical and physical sciences, however, were another matter. The once great Muslim tradition of scientific inquiry and experiment had long since atrophied and died, leaving a society strongly resistant to the scientific spirit. In the words of a Turkish historian of science, "The scientific current broke against the dykes of literature and jurisprudence."[3] No less serious an impediment was the deep-rooted social attitude toward power, work, and status that often makes the Middle Easterner, even today, a bold and resourceful driver but a reluctant and unpredictable mechanic. Medicine, engineering, and other useful sciences were taught at the very first military schools; scientific treatises were among the first Western works translated into Turkish and Arabic, but many medical graduates preferred to become administrators rather than soil their hands with patients, and the scientific schools remained alien and exotic growths in need of constant care and renewed graftings from the West. There was no real development of original scientific work, such as occurred in Japan, China, or India, and each generation of students had to draw again from the sources in the West, which had meanwhile itself been making immense progress. The result was that the disparity in scientific knowledge, technological capacity, and therefore of military power between the Middle East and the advanced countries of the West is greater now than it was two hundred years ago, when the whole process of Westernization began. This disparity was maintained and, indeed, aggravated by the reluctance or inability to make the social and cultural changes that are necessary to sustain a modern state of the Western type. The military consequences of this disparity were dramatically illustrated in the Gulf War of 1991.

From time to time, Middle Eastern thinkers have put the question: What is the result of all this Westernization? It is a question that we of the West may well ask ourselves, too. It is our complacent habit in the Western world to make ourselves the model of virtue and progress. To be like us is to be good; to be unlike us is to be bad. To become more like us is to improve; to become less like us is to deteriorate. It is not necessarily so. When civilizations clash, there is one that prevails and one that is shattered. Idealists and ideologues may talk glibly of "a marriage of the best elements" from both sides, but the usual result of such an encounter is a cohabitation of the worst.

The impact of the West in the Middle East has brought great benefits and will surely bring others—in wealth and comfort, knowledge and artifacts, and the opening of new ways that were previously shut. These are good roads, though it is not always certain where they lead.

Westernization—the work of Westerners and still more of Westernizers—has also brought changes of doubtful merit. One of these is the political disintegration and fragmentation of the region. Until modern times, there was an established political order in the Middle East, with the shah as ruler of Persia and the sultan as sovereign or suzerain of the rest. The sultan may not always have been loved by his subjects, but he was respected and, what is more important, accepted as the legitimate sovereign of the last of the Muslim universal empires. The sultan was overthrown and the empire destroyed. In his place came a succession of kings, presidents, and dictators who managed for a time to win the acclamation and support of their peoples, but never that spontaneous and unquestioning acceptance of their right to rule that the old legitimate sovereigns possessed and that dispensed them from the need for either violent repression or demagogic politics.

With the old legality and loyalty, the peoples of the Middle East also lost their ancient corporate identity. Instead of being members of a millennial Islamic imperial polity, they found themselves citizens of a string of dependencies and then nation-states, most of them entities new to history, often with borrowed or resurrected names, and only now beginning to strike roots in the consciousness and loyalties of their peoples.

The undermining and collapse of the old political order were accompanied by a parallel process of social and cultural disintegration. The old order may have been decayed, but it was still functioning, with a mutually understood system of loyalties and responsibilities binding together the different groups and classes of society. The old patterns were destroyed, the old values derided and abandoned; in their place a new set of institutions, laws, and standards was imported from the West, which for long remained alien and irrelevant to the needs, feelings, and aspirations of the Muslim peoples of the Middle East. It may well be that these changes were "necessary" and "inevitable," as these words are used by politicians and historians. The fact remains that they brought a period of formlessness and irresponsibility deeply damaging to Middle Eastern polity and society.

The economic consequences of Westernization are too well known to need more than a brief mention: the explosive rise in population, above all in Egypt, unaccompanied by any corresponding increase in food supply; the enormous new wealth derived from oil unevenly, even erratically, distributed both between and within countries; the widening and more visible gap between rich and poor; the creation of new appetites and ambitions, more rapidly than the means of satisfying them. The technological disparity remained, and successive Middle East wars revealed that buying advanced technological weaponry can do much damage, but does not create a technologically advanced army, still less a technologically advanced society. These tensions have been building up for some time past. In our day they have come to the breaking point.

The attitude of the peoples of the Middle East toward the West has gone through several phases. For many centuries, while Europe was rising to greater and greater heights of achievement, the East was sinking in the comfortable torpor of decay, unwilling and unable to perceive or to understand the vast changes that were taking place. In the nineteenth century, their illusions of superiority and self-sufficiency were finally shattered, and they awoke to a disagreeable reality in which their countries, their resources, their civilizations, their very souls were menaced by a Europe that was rich and powerful beyond belief and that, in its limitless self-confidence, aggressiveness, and acquisitiveness, seemed to be bringing the whole world within its grasp.

In this situation, the mood of the Easterner began to change from ignorant complacency to anxious emulation. The West was great and strong; by study and imitation, it might be possible to discover and apply the elusive secret of its greatness and strength, and generations of eager students and reformers toiled in the search. They may not have loved the West, or even understood it, but they did admire and respect it.

There came a time when many of them did neither. The mood of admiration and imitation gave way to one of envious rancor. This change was no doubt helped by the West's lamentable political and moral failures; it was also helped by the lessons of liberty and human self-respect that the West had taught. In the words of Muḥammad Iqbāl, in a poem addressed to England, on the desire of the Easterner for freedom:

> It was the scent of the rose that drew the
>   nightingale to the garden:
> Otherwise the nightingale would not even have
>   known that there was a garden.[4]

But most of all, the wave of hostility was due to the crisis of a civilization reacting at last against the impact of alien forces that had dominated, dislocated, and transformed it. It is some of these processes of impact, response, and reaction that must now claim our attention.

3

~~~~~~~~~~

The Quest for Freedom

In 1878 a young Turkish diplomat called Sadullah went to see the Great Exhibition in Paris. In a letter describing what he saw, he wrote:

> In front of the central gate there is a statue of freedom; she has a staff in her hand and is seated on a chair. Her style and appearance convey this message: "O worthy visitors! When you look upon this fascinating display of human progress, do not forget that all these achievements are the work of freedom. It is under the protection of freedom that peoples and nations attain happiness. Without freedom, there can be no security; without security, no endeavour; without endeavour, no prosperity; without prosperity, no happiness."[1]

Liberty, in other words, is an essential prerequisite to the pursuit of happiness, through the intermediate stages as indicated.

In these words, Sadullah was expressing a view common among Middle Eastern explorers of Europe in the nineteenth century: the view that political freedom was the secret source of Western power and success, the Aladdin's lamp with which the East might conjure up the genie of progress and win the fabulous treasures of the gorgeous and mysterious Occident.

At this point, some definition of terms is necessary. "Freedom" and "independence" are often loosely used as synonyms but should be differentiated. For the sake of clarity, we may, for the moment, define "freedom" as a political term referring to the position of the individual within the group—to the immunity of the citizen from arbitrary and illegal action by the authorities and to his right to participate in the formation and conduct of government. "Independence," on the other hand, refers to the position of the group in relation to other groups—to the formation and sovereignty of the state untrammeled by any superior, alien authority. Freedom and independence are thus quite different—sometimes even mutually exclusive—things and represent different objectives. Freedom is maintained and exercised through a form of political organization that is, by those who practice it, now usually called democracy. It is true that in modern times the word "democracy" has been used with many adjectives and in many other senses: social, organic, basic, guided, and popular; the neo-Marxist dictatorship of the secretariat; the unanimous plebiscitary ratification of military *res gestae*; royal affability and party public relations. Our present concern is with none of these but with free, representative and constitutional government and with the attempt to introduce such government in the Middle East. It has been, so far, a sad story.

The idea of political freedom first appeared in the Middle East at the end of the eighteenth century, grew and developed during the nineteenth, and, in most of the area, died out in the middle of the twentieth.

Despite the elective doctrines of the Muslim jurists, enshrining the memories of a remote nomadic past, the political experience of the Middle East under the caliphs and sultans was one of almost unrelieved autocracy, in which obedience to the sovereign was a religious as well as a political obligation, and disobedience a sin as well as a crime. But although the Muslim sovereign was an autocrat, he was not a pure despot. He was always subject, in theory and to a large extent even in practice, to the holy law of Islam. By the eighteenth century, the effective authority of the Ottoman sultan was limited by such entrenched and powerful groups as the ulema, the janissaries, and the provincial notables. There were, however, no established bodies to represent them. Islamic law knows no corporate legal persons; Islamic history shows no councils or communes, no synods or parliaments, nor any other kind of elected or representative assembly. It is interesting that the jurists never accepted the principle of majority decision. There was no point, since the need for a procedure of corporate, collective decision never arose. In heaven there was one God, and one alone; on earth there was no court but a single judge, no state but a single ruler.

This ancient tradition of autocracy and acquiescence was first breached by the impact of the ideas of the French Revolution. Interest was soon aroused. In April 1797 the English traveler W. G. Browne had a conversation with Ḥasan Junblāṭ, a Druze chief in Kasrawān, in the north Lebanon: "He was very inquisitive as to the motives and history of the French Revolution, and the present religious creed of that nation; on hearing the detail on which, he however made no interesting remarks."[2] In the following year, with the arrival of the French in Egypt, fuller and perhaps more stimulating details were available. In Turkey the ideas of the revolution became known even earlier and were actively propagated by the French embassy and its friends. On 14 July 1793, the French community had a solemn celebration at which they read the Declaration of the Rights of Man, swore allegiance to the republic, and drank the health of the French republic and Selim III, the soldiers of the motherland and the friends of liberty, and universal brotherhood. The inauguration of the republican flag the following year provided the occasion for a still bigger celebration, culminating in a salute from two French ships moored off Seraglio Point. The party ended with the guests dancing a republican *carmagnole* around the tree of liberty that had been planted in the soil of Turkey, on the grounds of the French embassy.

There is no evidence that the Turks were much interested in these proceedings. But the ideas that they represented began to percolate, at first in a very limited circle and then to larger and larger groups among the intellectual elite. The tree of liberty bore fruit. The French Revolution was the first great movement of ideas in Europe that was not expressed in more or less Christian terms, and its doctrines could therefore spread, unhampered, through the new channels that were being opened into the world of Islam. A new generation was to grow up fascinated by the ideals of liberty, equality, and fraternity. It was some time before their successors decided that the first two were mutually exclusive, and the third in need of redefinition.

The first step in the direction of constitutional government was taken as early as 1808, when the grand vizier Bayrakdar Mustafa Pasha convened an assembly of dignitaries and provincial lords and notables in Istanbul. After some negotiations, they signed—and made the sultan sign—a deed of agreement. Various interpretations have been placed on these events, which in any case came to nothing. Ad hoc consultative meetings, called *meshveret* (from the Arabic *mashwara*), were not uncommon in the Ottoman Empire. What was new and important was that the "deed of agreement" was a reciprocal contract negotiated between the Sultan and groups of his servants and subjects, in which the latter appear as independent contracting parties, receiving as well as conceding certain rights and privileges.

Consultation is recommended in the Qur'ān and was practiced from time to time by sovereigns with their counselors, officials, and courtiers. The nineteenth century brought the first attempts to extend and institutionalize it. The French had set an example by appointing several consultative bodies during their occupation of Egypt. In 1829 Muḥammad 'Alī Pasha set up a council of consultation (*majlis mashwara*) of 156 members, all nominated. They consisted of 33 high officials of the central government, 24 provincial officials, and 99 notables. They met only once a year, for a day or longer if necessary, and discussed such topics as agriculture, education, and taxes. When Muḥammad 'Alī occupied Palestine and Syria, his governors appointed a consultative council of notables (*majlis shūrā*) in each of the main towns, with advisory and some judicial functions. In 1845 the Ottoman sultan, Abdülmejid, also experimented with an assembly of provincial representatives. Two were to be chosen from each province, "from among those who are respected and trusted, are people of intelligence and knowledge, who know the requisites of prosperity and the characteristics of the population."[3] Despite these high qualifications the experiment produced no results and was abandoned. A similar and equally inconclusive experiment was held in Persia shortly after.

While sultans and pashas experimented with nominated advisory bodies, some of their subjects began to play with more radical ideas. In classical Islamic usage, *ḥurriyya* (freedom) was primarily a legal term denoting the legal status of the free person, as opposed to that of the slave. The first references to political freedom in Muslim writings are hostile and suspicious; it is something foolish and evil, much the same as libertinism and anarchy. But soon a more positive attitude appears. In the 1820s and 1830s, young Muslims began to travel to Europe in search of enlightenment and of the elusive secret of Western power. In the Europe of that time there was no lack of voices to commend the merits of liberalism, the cause of idealists and businessmen alike—and what, to the alien visitor, could have seemed more extraordinary, more distinctive of the West than constitutional and representative government? It is not surprising that many of them decided that this was the talisman they sought.

One of the first Middle Easterners to argue the merits of parliamentary government was an Egyptian, the Azhari Sheikh Rifāʿa Rāfiʿ al-Ṭahṭāwī. In 1826, at the age of twenty-five, he accompanied the Egyptian student mission to Paris and stayed there until 1831. He was not himself a member of the mission, but was their religious preceptor. He seems, however, to have learned more than did any of his wards. His book, containing an account of what he saw in France, was published in Arabic in 1834 and in a Turkish translation in 1839. It contains a description of parliamentary government, the purpose of which is to secure government under law and to protect the subjects from tyranny—or rather, as he acutely observes, to give the subjects the opportunity to protect themselves. Sheikh Rifāʿa witnessed and explained the 1830 revolution in which, he says, the king was removed for violating the constitution and attempting to curtail the freedoms that it ensured. He attached great importance to the press, "the sheets called newspapers [al-waraqāt . . . al-musammāt bi'l-jurnālāt wa'l-gāzeṭāt]"[4] as a safeguard against misrule and a medium for the communication of knowledge and ideas. The book includes a complete translation of the French constitution, with comments.

Sheikh Rifāʿa was no liberal revolutionary, but a loyal servant of Muḥammad ʿAlī and his successors, whom he served with distinction for many years. His political teachings, after his return to Egypt, tended to be cautious and conservative; the sovereign must rule as well as reign, but should use his power wisely and justly, with proper respect for the law and for the rights of the subject, a position closer to the enlightened despots than to the revolution. Such exhortations to the sovereign to govern with justice were in the classical tradition of Islamic political writings; what was new was the idea that the subject has a *right* to justice, and that some sort of apparatus might be set up to secure that right. The same kind of modified conservatism can be found in an essay written by Sadık Rıfat Pasha, the Turkish ambassador in Vienna in 1837, perhaps under the influence of Metternich. He too speaks of the "rights of the people" and "the rights of freedom," by which he meant freedom from oppressive and arbitrary government.[5]

But in fact the government was becoming more and not less oppressive. The creation of a modern administrative apparatus, on the one hand, and the introduction of modern methods of communication and coercion, on the other, were tightening the screws of government; the old limiting intermediate powers of the religious, military, and landowning interests were abrogated or enfeebled, leaving the state with nothing but its own edicts and charters to restrain it. Little understood by the people, halfheartedly applied by the officials, supported by no strong body of either interest or opinion, these charters of civil rights, however well intentioned, could have but little effect.

At this point a cleavage begins to appear between reformers and radicals—the Ottoman heirs of the Enlightenment and of the Revolution. The former, usually conservative and authoritarian in politics, sought to modernize in order to strengthen and enrich their countries, and used all the powers of the reinforced state for this purpose. The latter, including both reactionary and progressive elements, criticized the reforms and still more the manner of their application, and sought a remedy in constitutionalism, in ideas that they derived from European liberalism but often attributed to Qur'anic and other Islamic doctrines. These ideological differences were complicated—sometimes even motivated—by personal and political quarrels, and notably by the rivalry between Ottoman Istanbul and khedivial Cairo which, throughout the nineteenth and early twentieth centuries, was an important element in Middle Eastern political life.

In the 1860s and 1870s, constitutionalism in the Middle East seemed to be taking important steps forward. In 1861 the bey of Tunis, then an autonomous monarchy under a loose Ottoman suzerainty, proclaimed a constitution, the first in any Islamic country. The bey remained head of the state and the faith and retained executive power for himself and his ministers, with whom, however, he was responsible to a Grand Council of sixty members, some appointed by the bey and some co-opted, for a term of five years. The judicial power was to be exercised by an independent judiciary, the legislative power shared by the council with the government. The Tunisian constitution was suspended in 1864, but the trend continued elsewhere. The year 1866 brought important developments in other lands under Ottoman suzerainty, nearer home. In Romania, a liberal constitution was proclaimed, based on the Belgian constitution of 1831. In Egypt, the khedive Ismā'īl created a Consultative Assembly of Delegates (Majlis Shūrā al-Nuwwāb), consisting of seventy-five delegates elected for a three-year term by a system of indirect, collegiate elections. The Young Ottoman constitutionalists who in 1867 sought refuge in England and France received financial support from the khedive's brother, Mustafa Fazil Pasha, and then from the khedive Ismāʿīl himself. After some setbacks, their cause seemed to triumph, when in 1876 an Ottoman constitution was promulgated in Istanbul by the new sultan, Abdülhamid II. This too was influenced by the liberal monarchical Belgian constitution, both directly and through the Prussian constitutional enactment of 1850, in which Belgian liberal principles were adapted in a number of respects to the more authoritarian traditions of Prussia. It provided for a parliament, consisting of a nominated senate and an elected chamber, with some, rather perfunctory, recognition of the principle of the separation of powers.

The effective life of the constitution was brief. After a general election, the first Ottoman parliament assembled in March 1877 and sat until June. New elections were then held, and a second parliament met in December. It soon began to show alarming vigor, and on 14 February was summarily dismissed by the sultan. The first Ottoman parliament had sat for two sessions, of about five months in all; it did not meet again for thirty years.

These early constitutional reforms were not only gestures of emulation toward Europe; they also had a quality of propitiation. They were intended to prove that their authors were also civilized and progressive by European standards and therefore worthy of respect—to qualify for loans and other forms of favorable consideration and, in extreme cases, to ward off interference and occupation. In these purposes they secured only fitful and limited success. Neither the short-lived Tunisian constitution nor the slightly longer Egyptian parliamentary experiment did anything to halt the downward plunge to bankruptcy, disorder, control, and occupation. Some observers thought they might even have helped it. In Turkey, Sultan Abdülhamid, the last of the great authoritarian reformers of the nineteenth century, decided to dispense with the trappings of democracy and to achieve modernization by more traditional methods.

For the next thirty years, the only place in the Middle East where parliamentary institutions of any kind existed was Egypt. The assembly of 1866 held its prescribed three terms and was succeeded by further, similar assemblies, elected in 1869, 1876, and 1881. In 1882, during the ʿUrābī revolt, the assembly prepared and promulgated a draft parliamentary constitution. The draft was abrogated and the assembly dismissed when ʿUrābī failed. A new start was made after the British occupation of 1882, when Lord Dufferin, who was sent to Egypt to reorganize the government of the country, wrote to the foreign secretary, Lord Granville, in London that the

British occupation should be based on "national independence and constitutional government."[6] The first objective, because of changing circumstances, received less attention than it required, though more than is sometimes allowed. The second was a matter of continuing concern to the British authorities, in both London and Cairo, who made a serious attempt to place the government of the country on a constitutional basis and allowed the press a measure of freedom that, though limited, was sufficient to attract creative and critical writers from neighboring territories enjoying full independence but no freedom. The new Organic Law for Egypt, promulgated in May 1883, provided for two quasi-parliamentary bodies. The first was a legislative council of thirty members, fourteen nominated and permanent, sixteen indirectly elected for six years. The second, the General Assembly, consisted of the khedive's ministers, the members of the legislative council, and forty-six others elected for six years. These bodies, with their restricted and apathetic electorates, their limited and advisory powers, their brief and infrequent meetings, must have seemed a poor substitute for the constitutional aspirations of the liberals. They functioned, however, regularly and not altogether ineffectively, from 1883 to 1912 and were able on more than one occasion to take an independent line, asserting their views and rights against the khedive and sometimes against the occupying power. Their growing authority was recognized in 1913 when they were merged in a new and more powerful body, called the Legislative Assembly. This consisted of the ministers, seventeen nominated and sixty-six elected members, indirectly elected for a term of six years, one-third every two years. This rule of rotation was perhaps due to American influence. The first elections were in October 1913; the first session lasted from January to June 1914. There were no more elections or assemblies until after the war.

Meanwhile, far more radical developments had been taking place farther north. In 1905 a thrill of exultation passed through Asia when for the first time an Asian power, Japan, was able to defeat a European great power, Russia, in battle on both land and sea. There were some who made the further observation that the oriental victor was the only Asian country that had adopted a form of parliamentary and constitutional government, while the European loser was the only European power that had refused to do so. In Russia, the czar himself, faced with revolution, seemed to concede the point by granting a form of constitution and convening the first Duma. In Egypt, the nationalist leader Muṣṭafā Kāmil wrote a book called *The Rising*

Sun, showing by the example of Japan how an Oriental nation could achieve self-renewal and success. In Turkey, two officers wrote a five-volume illustrated history of the Russo-Japanese war, and a minor civil servant, who was also a part-time dervish, noted in his diary that his fervent prayers had helped achieve the Japanese victory. In Iran, in the summer of 1906, a constitutional revolution forced the shah to convene a national assembly which drafted a liberal constitution. Two years later, the Young Turk revolutionary officers, fearing—mistakenly as it turned out—that the meeting of the British and Russian sovereigns at Reval portended the demise of the Sick Man of Europe, decided on an immediate dose of the constitutional elixir and forced the reluctant sultan to restore the constitution of 1876, thus inaugurating the second, somewhat longer, and far stormier interlude of constitutional government in Turkey.

The victory of the allied and associated powers over their somewhat less democratic opponents in 1918, with the collapse of the only autocracy in the allied camp, seemed to provide final proof of the proposition that democracy makes a state healthy, wealthy, and strong. In Damascus, Prince Faysal's Syrian Congress drafted a constitution for a limited, parliamentary monarchy. It was abandoned with the arrival of the French on 19 July 1920. The British and French, as mandatary powers, created constitutional republics and monarchies in their own image in the countries under their control. Elsewhere, too, in the years following the victory, constitutions and parliaments spread all over the Middle East in what seemed a universal triumph of liberal and democratic principles.

Until very recently, it seemed that this great experiment had ended in almost unrelieved failure. The longest-lived constitutional regime in the Middle East was that of Iran, where the constitution promulgated after the liberal revolution of 1906 remained in force, though barely in effect, until the Islamic revolution of 1979, when it was formally abrogated. The oldest surviving parliamentary regime now is that of Lebanon, where the 1926 constitution, despite many vicissitudes and fairly drastic emendations, has remained technically in force, though civil war and external interference have undermined and perhaps nullified its working. Elsewhere, all the constitutions adopted in the democratic millennium of the 1920s were abandoned or replaced by more or less violent processes.

In Turkey, the will and the desire remain. Despite recurring crises at home, despite three military interventions since 1960, Turkey has retained its commitment to democratic values, and each of the three military regimes withdrew of its own free will and gave way to a restoration of constitutional and parliamentary government. Of the fifty-one member states of the Islamic Conference, Turkey alone qualifies as a stable democracy according to Samuel Huntington's simple but effective definition: a regime in which power has been transferred twice by means of elections.[7] The second transfer is of crucial importance. It may happen that a government in power, through either conviction or inadvertence, allows itself to be voted out of office. It would still remain to be seen whether those who succeed it would follow its example and be ready to depart by the same route by which they came.

In Iran, the victorious revolutionaries, along with proclaiming a return to ancient Islamic values, also promulgated a written constitution and established an elected legislative assembly, for neither of which is there any precedent in Islamic precept or practice. In the Islamic republic, elections are indeed contested, and there is some freedom of debate in the assembly and of comment in the press. These freedoms are, of course, subject to the acceptance of the basic principles of Islam and of the Islamic revolution as defined by its creators and their successors. The limits to freedom of discussion have never been clearly defined, but those who cross them are subject to swift and severe retribution.

The longest and, apart from Lebanon, the most successful record of a parliamentary government in the Arab world is that of Egypt. After the overthrow of the monarchy and the creation of a new republic by the "free officers" in the years 1952 to 1954, Egypt seemed once again to be setting an example to other Arab states, this time of the final and complete abandonment of the Western form of representative and liberal democracy. Since then, however, under President Nasser's successors, there has been a tentative return to contested elections for a representative assembly and to an opposition press free to criticize within certain well-understood limits.

A brief experiment with a written constitution and an elected assembly in Kuwait was terminated by the rulers sometime before the Iraqi invasion of 1990. More recently, there have been experiments with contested elections and critical newspapers in both Jordan and Algeria. In the latter country, in January 1992, the opposition Islamic Fundamentalist Front was even able to gain a significant electoral victory. It was not, however, allowed to enjoy it, and a new emergency regime was installed in office. Except in Turkey, critics were not permitted to criticize the ruling personalities or the basic policies that they followed, nor were opposition groups, however

large, permitted to vote their rulers out of power. Given the nature
of these oppositions, this limitation was not necessarily undemo-
cratic, since it is often clear that even if the rulers were to allow
themselves to be voted out of power, the victors would not repeat
the same error. In general, the captains and the kings still divide the
Arab lands, and neither show any inclination to depart.

Besides Turkey, there is one other continuously functioning democracy in the region: Israel, which in many respects presents a
curious anomaly. Israel is not an Islamic state and has not suffered
the disruptions and upheavals endured by its neighbors. Yet at first
sight, there seems little to encourage the development of Western-
style democratic institutions. The majority of Israel's citizens came
from countries with little or no democratic tradition or experience—
in Central and Eastern Europe, the Middle East, and North Africa.
Since the establishment of the state in 1948, Israel has been in a
continuous state of war with all or most of its neighbors, a condition
frequently leading to armed hostilities. In the areas under its rule
and even within its original frontiers, it rules over a large population
related by language, religion, culture, and sympathies to those same
neighbors. In such a predicament, the military inevitably plays a
large role, and in a region where military takeovers are the norm, it
might have been expected that sooner or later the Israeli generals—
or colonels—would follow the pattern of the region and seize power,
the more so since the Israeli electoral system of proportional rep-
resentation, with its unhappy record of petty squabbling, factional
pressures, precarious coalitions, and recurring deadlock, might have
made such a takeover seem defensible and even desirable. This did
not happen, however, and Israel remains, despite, or perhaps because
of, its state of perpetual semimobilization, an aggressively civilian
polity.

There have thus been only three countries in the modern Middle
East where political democracy has functioned with any success and
for any length of time—Israel, Lebanon, and Turkey. They are also
the three most European states in the area—the first, non-Islamic;
the second, only half-Islamic; and the third, wholly Islamic but with
a long record of Westernization and secularism. This has led some
observers to conclude that Islam and democracy are incompatible—
that is, that there is something in the Islamic pattern of social and
political behavior that impedes or prevents the proper working of
parliamentary institutions. In support of this thesis, they point to
the mishaps and breakdowns of parliamentary government in the
Islamic states, old and new, where it has been tried, including even

Pakistan, where its collapse was in striking contrast with the vigorous democracy of India, another successor state of the same imperial regime.

The quest for freedom in the Middle East, as elsewhere, has been primarily and most publicly concerned with familiar and recognizable political aims: the rights of the nation against foreign overlords and, more recently, the rights of the individual against the nation and those who rule it. At the same time, there has been another, parallel quest, less discussed yet more controversial and, on the whole, rather more successful—the quest for social freedom, specifically for the enfranchisement of the disenfranchised elements in society. In principle, Islam is strongly egalitarian, and Muslim scripture and tradition explicitly reject and denounce any form of inherited social privilege. Rank and honor are to be determined by merit, piety, and personal achievement and not by descent, whether racially or socially defined. But in fact, Muslims, like others, were anxious to transmit to their children what success they had achieved, and there was thus a recurring tendency to create new elites, based on power and wealth and upheld by birth and status. The resulting social inequalities arose in spite of, not because of, Islam, and until very recent times the social barriers between classes were always less rigid and more permeable than in Christian Europe.

But while inequalities by class or status were in principle rejected, and in practice softened, by Islamic teaching, there were other inequalities that were not merely sanctioned, but were imposed and regulated by the holy law of Islam. These are the three basic inequalities: between man and woman, believer and unbeliever, and free and slave.

The struggles for the removal of these three inequalities developed along very different lines and achieved sharply contrasting results. The struggle for independence, though in part inspired by foreign ideas, arose from inside and was directed against foreign oppressors. The struggle for emancipation for all three groups of inferiors was entirely inspired, and in large measure conducted, by foreigners and was directed against an authority that was indigenous and rooted in the society.

The progress of the three emancipations was very uneven. Two causes, the granting of equal rights to followers of other religions and the abolition of the slave trade and, ultimately, of slavery, were actively promoted by the European powers, the former by the combined diplomacy of the concert of Europe and the latter by the forceful intervention of the Royal Navy. Both were helped by a growing awareness among significant groups of Muslims that these inequalities damaged the reputation of their religion and culture in the eyes of the Western world, which had only recently, and rather incompletely, renounced both and was still feeling militantly virtuous in consequence.

In earlier times, the Islamic record for religious tolerance had been considerably better than that of Christendom. But the great wars of religion that almost destroyed Europe had left a new tolerance, bred of desperation, and a new secular definition of identity, authority, and allegiance. By the nineteenth century, deviant Christians and even non-Christians in the more enlightened parts of Europe enjoyed most, though perhaps not all, the rights of citizenship, and their position was notably better than that of non-Muslims in the Muslim states, which had not changed significantly for centuries.

In any case, in a world dominated by the Christian powers of Europe, these powers found it unacceptable that Christians anywhere should be accorded an inferior status. In part because of European pressure—but at least to an equal extent because of a rising tide of liberal sentiment at home—first Turkey and then other Muslim countries enacted legislation or promulgated constitutions declaring the equality of all religious communities before the law. In practice, it did not always work out, and both Western emissaries and native Christians from time to time received sharp reminders that it was not wise to go beyond what public opinion was prepared to accept. There were times and places when the non-Muslim subjects of the Muslim states were worse off after emancipation than before. The old status given to them under Islamic law, with limited but well-established and universally recognized rights, had been abolished. The new status as equal citizens meant less and less in a situation in which citizenship itself was losing all meaning.

Islam, like every other religion and civilization known to human history, accepted slavery as a fact of life and, like Christianity and Judaism, made some attempt to lessen its asperities. Muslim scripture and tradition urge humane treatment for the slave and recommend manumission as a meritorious act. In a rule without precedent in the ancient or medieval worlds, Islam prohibited the enslavement of free Muslims and even of free non-Muslims belonging to the tolerated communities under Muslim rule. This meant that the slave population could be recruited only by birth, since the children of slaves were born slaves, or by acquisition from outside the Islamic lands, by either tribute or purchase. Since a slave population adequate to perceived needs could not, as in ancient societies, be provided from domestic resources, slaves had to imported from elsewhere. Thus, by a sad paradox, one of the great humanizing reforms brought by the advent of Islam led to an expansion of slave raiding and slave trading beyond the frontiers, in Europe, Asia, and, above all, Africa.

Slaves were sometimes used for economic purposes—for example, in mines and on plantations—but they did not constitute the principal labor force of the Islamic world. Their major employment was in a wide variety of domestic and menial purposes and also, perhaps more especially, in the home as servants, concubines, or eunuchs. The last named were needed in considerable numbers in palaces and the wealthier households and also for the maintenance and protection of sacred places.

While enjoining kindly treatment and commending manumission, Islamic law and custom provided no basis for the abolition of slavery or even for the curtailment of the slave trade. From time to time, Muslim jurists inveighed against the misdeeds of the slave traders, especially their practice, contrary to Islamic law, of enslaving free black Muslims in Africa merely because they were black. In the nineteenth century, voices are heard for the first time expressing unhappiness about the institution as such. But the main impetus for reform came from the Western powers, which intervened, often forcefully, to prevent the capture of slaves in Africa and their export to the Middle East and Asia. Legal abolition for long remained impossible in countries still formally under Islamic law, and so it was confined to the actions taken by the British, French, and later Italian empires in the territories under their authority. The Ottoman Empire, however, under the pressure of both foreign and domestic opinion, took serious steps to reduce and, as far as possible, eliminate the slave trade, which by the last decades of the Ottoman Empire survived only in those areas, like Arabia and Libya, where Ottoman control was weakest.

The formal legal abolition of slavery was enacted in most of the remaining countries of the region in the period between the First and Second World Wars, and slave laws appear to have remained in force only in the Arabian peninsula and parts of Africa. The circumstances of the Second World War and the vicissitudes of postimperial politics seem to have permitted some small revival of slave trading, but the process of legal abolition continued and was in effect completed. The last major slave-owning societies in Southwest Asia—

Yemen and Saudi Arabia—both abolished slavery in 1962. Mauritania, where slavery was reintroduced after the ending of French rule in 1960, formally abolished it in 1980.

Western public opinion, with the effective support of Western power, on the one hand, and an increasing body of enlightened domestic public opinion in Muslim countries, on the other, contributed significantly—indeed decisively—to the legal emancipation of the non-Muslim and of the slave. In the great days of emancipation, however, neither Western nor Muslim liberals seem to have been much concerned with the third category of legally established inferiors—women. Yet in some ways their position was the worst of the three. A slave could be, and often was, liberated; a non-Muslim, could, if he chose, embrace Islam. Manumission and conversion alike legally terminated the state of inferiority. No such option was open to the woman. Women were also vastly more numerous and more important than either slaves or infidels, and their emancipation could cause a major disruption in the whole structure of society. The movement for women's rights, when it eventually appeared, though inspired by Western ideas, was entirely Muslim in its leadership and execution.

Some progress was made. A very small number of Muslim countries abolished polygamy, either by law or de facto, and a very few others imposed severe restrictions. But in most Muslim countries, while concubinage was in principle eliminated with the abolition of slavery, polygamy, child marriage, and divorce by repudiation remained legally and often socially permissible. Polygamy and child marriage, both abolished by the shah, were restored by the Islamic Republic in Iran. In general, the movement for the emancipation of women has achieved less and been more seriously threatened by the rise of fundamentalism than has either of the other two.

The emancipation of women has become a major theme in the writing and preaching of Islamic fundamentalists of all kinds. It figures in a prominent place, often in first place, among the evils that they denounce and intend to put right. Fundamentalists have paid much less attention to the other two. The revival of slavery is limited, surreptitious, and illegal, and no one has so far spoken out on its behalf. Non-Muslims have felt, and sometimes actually been threatened by fundamentalists, but except for specific local cases, this does not rank high on the fundamentalists' public agenda. The position of women does, however, and women have been the main sufferers wherever fundamentalists rule or even exert influence. It may well be that women, who have the most to lose from reaction and the most to gain from liberalizing reform, will yet be the strongest supporters of the nascent democracies of the Islamic world.

"Semites," says T. E. Lawrence, "have no half-tones in their register of vision . . . they exclude compromise, and pursue the logic of their ideas to its absurd ends."[8] That there is something in this, no observer of Middle Eastern affairs can deny. But those who go on to argue that Arabs and other Muslims are necessarily incapable of democratic government are surely guilty of the same kind of absurdity. Some features of traditional Islamic civilization, such as tolerance, social mobility, and respect for law, are distinctly favorable to democratic development. Classical Islam succeeded, as Christendom never really did, in combining religious tolerance with deep religious faith, extending it not only to unbelievers, but also— a far more exacting test—to heretics. The coexistence of differing schools of holy law, all regarded as orthodox, is another example of Islamic tolerance and compromise. Socially, Islam has always been democratic or, rather, egalitarian, rejecting both the caste system of India and the aristocratic privilege of Europe. It needed no revolution to introduce the "career open to the talents" to the Islamic world; it was there from the start, and despite the inevitable tendency to the formation of aristocracies, it was never really eliminated. Islamic theory has always insisted on the supremacy of the law and on the subordination to it of the sovereign. In the Ottoman Empire, the hierarchy of the ulema achieved considerable success in enforcing this principle. There remained, of course, the political difficulty—the total absence, despite the elective doctrine of the jurists, of any conception or experience of representative or limited government of any kind. It is this, no doubt, that underlies the theory that democracy cannot work in Islamic lands. That there is a predisposition to autocratic government among Muslim peoples is clear enough; that there is an inherent incapacity for any other has yet to be proved.

There is always something disquieting about a hypothesis that presumes a kind of political original sin in human societies. This one is, in any case, unnecessary, for there is enough in the recent history of the Middle East to explain the failure of constitutional democracy, without recourse to political theology. It is easy and tempting for Westerners to adopt an attitude of superiority, contemptuous or tolerant, and to ascribe the breakdown of distinctive Western institutions among other peoples to the lack on their part of some of the West's distinctive virtues. It is easy, but it is not wise, and certainly not helpful. Most Westerners no doubt share the belief that liberal democracy, with all its weaknesses, is the best instrument that any section of the human race has yet devised for the conduct of its political affairs. At the same time, they should remain aware of its local origin and character and try to avoid the primitive arrogance of making their own way of life the universal standard of political morality. "He is a barbarian," says Caesar of Britannus, the British slave, in Shaw's *Caesar and Cleopatra*, "and thinks that the customs of his tribe and island are the laws of nature." Political democracy is a good custom. It has already spread far from its native land and in time will surely spread much farther. It is not, however, a law of nature and in some areas has been tried, found wanting, and abandoned. We must ask why.

In the Middle East, a serious attempt was made to introduce and operate liberal democracy, with written constitutions, elected sovereign parliaments, judicial safeguards, a multitude of parties, and a free press. With few and atypical exceptions, these experiments have failed. In some countries, democratic institutions are in a state of disrepair or collapse; in others, they have already been abandoned, and the search has begun for other paths to the pursuit of happiness.

Today, with the hindsight of history to guide us, we can see many of the causes clearly enough. A political system taken ready-made not merely from another country but from another civilization, imposed by Western or Westernized rulers from above and from without, could not respond adequately to the strains and stresses of Islamic, Middle Eastern society. Democracy was installed by autocratic decree; parliament sat in the capital, operated and supported by a minute minority whose happy immersion in the new game of parties, programs and politicians was ignored or else watched with baffled incomprehension by the great mass of the people. The result was a political order unrelated to the past or present of the country and irrelevant to the needs of its future. The parliament at Westminster is the result of centuries of history, with its roots in the Anglo-Saxon *witenagemot*; it is the apex of a pyramid of self-governing institutions, with its base at the parish pump. It was evolved by Englishmen on the basis of English experience to meet English needs. The parliament of Cairo was imported in a box, to be assembled and put into use without even a set of do-it-yourself instructions. It responded to no need or demand of the Egyptian people; it enjoyed the backing of no powerful interest or body of opinion.

When a piece of expensive imported machinery falls apart in our hands, we are apt to lay the blame not on our own inexpert handling, but on the manufacturers and suppliers. The West, which acted in both capacities, has had perhaps more than its fair share of blame for the breakdown of democracy. It cannot, however, wholly disclaim responsibility. One fault was the failure to support adequately those who were its most enthusiastic disciples. Another lies in the mandatary system, which was supposed to provide training in responsibility, but instead gave advanced training in irresponsibility. The position was, if anything, worse in those countries that remained nominally independent, but subject to constant interference. There is a case to be made for as well as against the imperial peace— Persian, Roman, Arab, Turkish, French, or British—as a stage in the development and spread of civilizations. There is little that can be said in defense of the so-called imperialism encountered by the Middle East in the first half of the twentieth century—an imperialism of interference without responsibility, which would neither create nor permit stable and orderly government. Perhaps one of the most significant distinctions in the ex-imperial countries of Asia and Africa is between those that were directly administered through a colonial or imperial civil service and those that were under some form of indirect rule or influence. The people of the latter group of countries got the worst of both worlds, receiving neither the training in administration of the colonial territories nor the practice in responsibility of the old independent states. The system of direct rule, apart from the useful legacy of an efficient modern bureaucracy, often has the additional merit of clarity. In British India, for example, the transfer of power and responsibility was clear, precise, and unequivocal. Until 15 August 1947, the British were responsible; thereafter, the British ceased to be and the Indians became responsible, and no serious observer has claimed or suspected otherwise. In Algeria, a long and hard-fought war with a decisive result achieved a similar clarity. In Egypt, it would be difficult to agree on the date of the effective transfer of responsibility within half a century. This situation, with its parallels in other Middle Eastern countries, produced a generation of politicians more apt to demand responsibility than to accept it, with a tendency to take refuge from reality that has not entirely died out. This finds expression in an addiction to conspiracy theories: to avoid any serious critical examination of their own societies and even policies and, instead, to place all blame for all evil on former imperial masters and on current enemies, both open and secret. The first at least, forty years after the ending of imperial rule, lacks even minimal plausibility. There are too many leaders who are willing to profit from that most insidious form of

Western prejudice that shows itself by expecting and accepting a lower standard of behavior and performance.

There is, of course, more to the question of democratic viability than cultural traditions and political aptitudes. Israel and pre–civil war Lebanon, two of the exceptions to the record of failure, are not only culturally Westernized; they are also relatively well fed, well clothed, and well housed. A small and highly urbanized population in a small area, with good communications and a high standard of education and of living, gives democracy a better chance than do the sprawling impoverished peasant slums that make up a good deal of the rest of the Middle East. After Israel and Lebanon, Turkey has the highest per capita income, the greatest mileage of railway in relation to area, the highest rate of literacy in the Middle East— although Egypt has more industry, more town dwellers, and until recently had more newspaper readers. There would seem to be some correlation between democracy and material progress, but which is the chicken and which is the egg is another question.

This much can be said with reasonable certainty: that many of the social and economic factors that helped make democracy work in other parts of the world are missing in the Middle East, or at least were missing in the crucial period when the experiment was tried. Society was still composed mainly of landlords and peasants. The commercial and industrial middle class, such as it was, consisted largely of foreigners and members of minorities, who as such were unable to play the classical political and cultural role of the bourgeoisie in Western societies. The new, Muslim professional class of lawyers, journalists, and teachers lacked the economic power and cohesive force to play any really independent role. The industrial working class barely existed; the peasant masses and urban *lumpenproletariat* were poor, ignorant, and unorganized, still unfitted for participation in political life. In such a society, no new and greater loyalty could arise to transcend the old and intense loyalties to tribe, clan, and family, to sect and guild; no tradition of local cooperation and initiative could develop to break the ancient habits of dependence and acquiescence. The liberals tried and failed, and the parliamentary system passed into the hands of those who controlled wealth and could command or buy obedience. They used it chiefly as an instrument to maintain their own power and to prevent any change or reform that they considered a threat to their interests.

In a long period of tranquillity, the peoples of the Middle East might perhaps have managed to adjust their imported political structures to their own conditions and needs. No such period was allowed to them. Instead, their young and untried democracies were subjected to a series of violent political shocks and stresses, of both internal and external origin, and confronted with the familiar Afro-Asian economic problem of the demographic explosion. In most countries, the parliamentary system collapsed under the strain. All too often, the disappointment and frustration of leaders gave way to a cynicism and opportunism that outraged the moral and religious sense of those whom they professed to lead and brought the whole institution of liberal democracy into disrepute. For the average Egyptian, representative government meant not Westminster or Washington, but Fārūq and the pashas, and who could blame him if he rejected and despised it?

For a while, the ideal of democracy was replaced by another, that of republicanism. There was a time when republic and democracy were thought to be two different ways of saying the same thing; modern Greek indeed makes the word *demokratia* do service for both. Today, of course, we know better. In an age of democratic monarchies and authoritarian republics, we are unlikely to confuse the two. Republic and democracy, far from being synonymous, seem barely compatible in many parts of the world.

In the Middle East, republicanism has not always been associated with libertarian ideas. The first Muslim republics were established in the Turkic territories of the Russian Empire, where the temporary relaxation of pressure from the center after the revolution of 1917 allowed an interval of local experimentation. In some areas, notably in Azerbaijan, this took the form of bourgeois nationalist republics, all of which were in due course conquered by the Red Army and incorporated into the Soviet Union. The Kemalist republic in Turkey and the French-style republics in Syria and Lebanon set new patterns, but it was not until after the Second World War that a new wave of republicanism was launched with the proclamation, by the military regime, of the Egyptian republic, in June 1953. This was followed by a number of others, not all of the same kind: Pakistan, an Islamic republic, in November 1953; the Sudan in 1956; Iraq, by revolution, in 1953; Tunisia in 1959; Yemen in 1962; Libya in 1969; and Iran in 1979. Today all but a handful of the states of the Middle East are called republics, although the common designation covers a wide variety of political realities. In Middle Eastern usage, a republic is a state with a non-dynastic head. The term has no reference to the processes by which the head attains his office, or to the manner in which he discharges it. Republicanism meant the end of monarchy and of much—though not all—that was connected with it. It had nothing to do with representative government or liberal democracy.

While democracy faltered and died in the Arab lands, the quest for freedom entered on new paths. Individual freedom was not a major issue during the period of Anglo-French and other, later, foreign domination. Although limited in various ways, it was on the whole more extensive and better protected than at any time before or since. What was far more important was the demand for corporate or collective freedom, more technically known as independence. The British and French empires, by the logic of their own systems rather than in response to popular demand, conceded a large measure of freedom, but withheld independence. It was natural, therefore, that the national political struggle should have concentrated on the latter and neglected the former. The ending of imperial rule was the focus and purpose of all political effort, never more so than in the period just after it was ended. With the coming of independence, it was found that freedom—in the old, classical liberal sense—had been lost. There were few to resist or lament its passing.

The ending of foreign rule, when it came, did not solve but merely revealed the fundamental economic, social, and political problems of the Arab lands. Imperialism, though repeatedly vanquished, remained the chief enemy, but with it another was associated—feudalism, sometimes also called capitalism. Both terms designated the existing economic order. A period of experiment and upheaval followed, a period of policies described by their friends as pragmatic, by their enemies as opportunist. And then, in the summer of 1961, the government of the United Arab Republic revealed the name of the new ideology that was to be their guiding light. It was called Arab socialism, and its purpose was to secure economic liberty, the only kind that mattered. "Today," said President Nasser, announcing a series of nationalizations,

> we are experiencing real economic liberty. No one exercises arbitrary power over the economy of the country or over its inhabitants. Every citizen feels that he is free in his country on the economic level and that he is not subjected to the dictatorship of capital.... True liberty is true democracy. It is economic liberty and social equality.

A few days earlier, the president had given his definition of democracy:

Fundamentally, democracy means the establishment of social justice and equity for the oppressed class as against the oppressive class. Fundamentally, democracy means that government should not be the monopoly of feudalism and exploiting capital, but should be for the welfare of the whole nation.... Democracy is not created simply by issuing a constitution or setting up a parliament. Democracy is not defined by the constitution or the parliament, but is created by eliminating feudalism and monopoly and the domination of capital. There is no freedom and no democracy without equality, and no equality with feudalism and exploitation and domination by capital.[9]

Like "freedom," like "democracy," "socialism" is a word of many meanings. The Soviet Union, we were told, was dedicated to the building of socialism; so too are the British and Scandinavian Labour parties. One of the most famous of parties bearing the name socialist was the National Socialist German Workers' party, usually known by its German abbreviated name as the Nazis. In the demonology of the American radical right—it has been said—socialism means anything to the left of Louis XIV. According to the rector of Al-Azhar, in a statement published on 22 December 1961, the most perfect, complete, useful, and profound socialism is that prescribed by Islam and resting on the foundations of the faith. To which of these, if any, is Arab socialism related?

Socialism began in the Middle East with small coteries, as a more recondite version of the prevailing fashion of copying Europe. A few serious writers gave it their support, such as the Syrian Christian Shiblī Shumayyil (1860–1917) and the Egyptian Christian Salāma Mūsā (ca. 1887–1959). Both followed Western models of socialism: Shumayyil, the French school of Jaurès; Mūsā, the English Fabians. Also French in inspiration was the short-lived and ineffectual Ottoman Socialist party, founded in 1910, with a branch in Paris and a newspaper called *Besheriyet* (Humanity). The Russian Revolution brought a brief spurt of left-wing socialist activities in several countries, but this too petered out in sectarian squabbling, leaving only a very small, very hard core of professional revolutionaries. In mandatary Palestine, a strong social-democratic labor movement, of European type, developed among the Jewish population. Elsewhere in the Middle East in the 1920s and 1930s, socialism had virtually no following—nothing, for example, that could be compared with the social and political radicalism of the nationalist movements in India and Southeast Asia.

A new phase began with the triumph of Soviet arms and the

electoral victory of the British Labour party in 1945. The Soviets, it seemed, had won the war, and even in Britain the people had preferred socialism to Churchill. Socialism might therefore be a good thing. In addition, it seemed to provide an answer for the mounting economic problems of the area. A series of socialist parties appeared in various countries, the most important of which was Akram Ḥaurānī's Arab Socialist party, founded in Syria in 1950. In 1953 it was amalgamated with Michel ʿAflaq's Arab Renaissance party, to form the Arab Socialist Renaissance party, usually known as the Baʿth. The nucleus of the party was a group formed in 1941 in Vichy-occupied Syria to mobilize sympathy and support for the short-lived pro-Axis regime of Rashīd ʿAlī in Iraq. The ideological writings of its founders clearly reflect the ideas of that time and place. Later, the party underwent some changes and, with a program combining economic socialism and a kind of mystical nationalism, soon won a considerable following in the Arab East. Apart from the Communists, it was the only party with a systematic ideology, an extensive network of branches, and a following among both the intellectuals and the working classes. In 1956 the Baʿth leaders joined the government in Syria, and were instrumental in taking that country into the United Arab Republic. For a while, the Baʿth played a predominant role in Syria after the union and claimed even to be providing ideological leadership for the UAR itself. By the end of 1959, however, they were losing ground. In Iraq, Jordan, and Lebanon they were opposed and, on occasion, suppressed. Even in the UAR, their leaders were dismissed from the high federal offices that they had held, and the party itself was suppressed twenty-two months after the union. The Baʿth did not return to prominence until the spring of 1963, when the revolutions in Iraq and Syria brought it to power in both countries and inaugurated a new sequence of both collaboration and conflict with President Nasser. In the meantime, the only place where socialist ideology could be seriously discussed was liberal, capitalist Beirut.

Socialism was in the air in the 1950s, just as fascism had been in the 1930s and 1940s, and liberalism a century earlier. Like its predecessor, socialism won a certain following among intellectuals, but it was not they who brought it to power. The socialist revolution, like the liberal constitutions, was imposed from above—not in response to a popular demand, not by the victory of a socialist or working-class movement, but by the decision of a military regime that had already been in power for nine years. Some practical steps, of a nondoctrinal nature, had been taken earlier in Egypt. British,

French, and some Jewish enterprises had been nationalized following the Sinai and Suez expeditions; Belgian assets were added during the Congo crisis. The resulting flight of foreign and minority capital narrowed the field of candidates for what one might call conservative nationalizations. The government, apparently despairing of private enterprise, decided to adopt a more active role in economic life. Statements of the time refer to social justice rather than to socialism and appear to envisage a kind of limited state capitalism with a welfare program. By 1960, socialism was becoming more explicit in both word and deed, particularly with the nationalization of the great Miṣr group of enterprises. The nationalization of the newspaper press in the same year was not purely, or even primarily, an economic measure.

The next stage in Egypt came with the series of decrees in July 1961, establishing state ownership or control over almost all large-scale economic enterprises, taking over, with compensation, all landholdings above a hundred feddans (about a hundred acres), imposing drastic income taxes in the higher brackets, and forbidding any individual to own more than £E10,000 worth of shares in a list of named companies. At the same time, a series of speeches and articles explained the nature and purpose of these measures and of the Arab socialism that they exemplified. The need of the country, said Muḥammad Ḥasanayn Haykal in an authoritative ideological article, was for a comprehensive plan harnessing the entire energy of the nation, which would ensure the necessary increase in production while providing for the immediate consumer needs of the long-deprived masses. In this way, both economic growth and social welfare would be achieved without either the domestic and colonial exploitation of Western capitalism or the ruthless sacrifice of the present to future generations, as practiced by Stalin and Mao Tse-tung.[10] A French politician once said that war is too serious a matter to be left to the generals. The Egyptian officers had already decided that politics was too important to be left to politicians; they now also reached the conclusion that business was too important a matter to be left to businessmen.

"Archaeology," said Bernard Berenson, "like all studies pursued with a scientific method, is based on comparison. It is constantly comparing unknown with known, uncertain with certain, unclassified with classified."[11] It is no doubt in pursuit of the archaeological method, which has served so well in the study of earlier periods of Middle Eastern history, that many attempts have been made to explain and categorize recent Middle Eastern developments by comparing them with earlier, already categorized events, which took place at other times or in other places.

Arab socialism, the dominant ideology of the 1950s, 1960s, and 1970s, has been subjected to several such explanations by comparison. Some have sought precedents in the Egyptian past, for there is also an indigenous tradition of state economic action, exemplified in the commercial monopolies of the Mamluk sultans in the fifteenth century and the land nationalization of Muḥammad 'Ali Pasha at the beginning of the nineteenth. Others have looked for Western parallels and, pronouncing a kind of guilt by association, have at different times described the military regime as Nazi and as Communist. To call a movement Nazi, in both the West and the Soviet Union, in most of Asia and Africa, was usually considered an insult. It was not so in the eastern Arab lands, where many leaders made no secret of their wartime sympathy and even association with the Axis. When Qāsim called Nasser a Hitlerite, the name was a danger sign of Communist penetration in Baghdad. This was not part of the Arab vocabulary of abuse, and its appearance as such was evidence of alien influence. In Egypt there were many reports, especially in the 1950s and 1960s (in Syria, not until much later), of the employment of Nazi German experts, particularly in police and propaganda work. The pervasive efficiency of the one and the strident mendacity of the other may well have owed something to the example or instruction of Nazi specialists. President Nasser himself on one occasion cited and recommended the so-called *Protocols of the Elders of Zion*.[12]

Nevertheless, one should not attach too much importance to this. Others, on both sides of the Iron Curtain, did not scruple to make use of Nazi experts in different fields when it suited them to do so. Evil communications corrupt good manners. These Nazi associations would seem to indicate a degree of moral obtuseness in the Egyptian regime of a kind that is fairly widespread in the modern world, but not necessarily any greater resemblance to the Nazi dictatorship than is implied in that.

Charges of communism also rest on rather slender foundations. The Communists, like the Nazis, could count on a sympathetic welcome, for they appeared in the same guise—as enemies of the West. For several decades after the end of the Second World War, Communism, unlike Nazism, was a fact, not a memory, and this meant both opportunity and danger. There was a period when Communist influence in the Arab world appeared to be great and growing. But in time, both the activities of the Soviet government in the Arab world and a closer acquaintance among Arabs with Soviet realities at home combined to reduce the attraction of this political and economic creed.

For a while, there was considerable debate in the Arabic world between the proponents of "Arab socialism," seen as both more authentic and more humane, and "scientific socialism," another name for Marxist Communism, defended by its supporters as superior to the corrupt and ineffectual local imitation and as offering the only true path to an ideal society. By the early 1990s, both brands had been thoroughly discredited. "Scientific socialism" had failed most dismally and dramatically in its countries of origin, while Arab socialism was believed by more and more observers to have prevented rather than produced the promised economic development and to have led the polities of the Arab world away from both traditional Arab tolerance and Western political democracy toward a string of totalitarian dictatorships patterned after the most odious of Central and Eastern European models.

It is no doubt tempting to try to explain Middle Eastern phenomena in terms of European or North or South American experience; it may also, within limits, be very useful. But on the whole, such comparisons—perhaps analogies would be a better word—obscure more than they explain. No doubt, Middle Eastern societies and politics are subject to the same human vicissitudes and therefore to the same rules of interpretation as those of the West. But since the Middle East has for some time now been under the influence of the West and has adopted Western outward forms in the organization and expression of its political and social life, it is fatally easy for the Western observer to take these alien outward forms as the element of comparison and to disregard or misrepresent the deeper realities that they so imperfectly express. The Islamic society of the Middle East, with its own complex web of experience and tradition, cannot adequately be labeled and classified with a few names and terms borrowed from the Western past.

In the meantime, events in the outside world once again, as so often before in this century, gave a new impetus and a new direction to the quest for freedom in the Middle East. The breakup of the Soviet bloc and then even of the Soviet Union, the retreat and perhaps the collapse of Soviet power, and, behind these, the manifest failure of the Communist system and its utter inability to make good on its promises, all had an immediate and obvious impact on the balance of power, both regional and international. More important, they also provoked some fundamental rethinking of aspirations and possibilities—similar, though on a much greater scale, to the new impulses generated by the Japanese victory over Russia in 1905, the Allied victory in 1918, the rise of fascism and Nazism in the interwar period, and the perceived Soviet victory in 1945. This time, the ending of the Cold War and the victory of the West were connected with such basic Western ideas as an open society, a market economy, and the maintenance of human rights, now at last defined in individual and not merely in national terms. In recent decades, in the Middle East as in Eastern Europe, the words "democracy" and "democratic" were sadly misused and came to connote—in the eyes of those who lived under the regimes that arrogated these terms— the economics of poverty enforced by the politics of tyranny. In the early 1990s, they acquired once again—in the eyes of those who looked at them from the outside—a connotation of freedom and plenty. It remains to be seen how far these newly defined democratic aspirations will accord with the economic, social, and political realities of the region and with the deep-rooted national and religious traditions of its peoples. One of the great dangers to freedom is the widespread belief—in the region and elsewhere—that general elections with universal suffrage are the foundation of democracy. They are not; they are the copestone, to be added when everything else is in place.

The fight for national freedom has been fought and won, though the triumph of nationalism over imperialism has become a new kind of Middle Eastern myth in need of seasonal and ritual reenactment. The fight for political freedom has been fought and lost, though this defeat need not be final. The fight for economic freedom—meaning freedom from want—has been engaged, and after severe setbacks and many self-inflicted wounds, there are signs, still very tentative, of a move in new directions and a readiness to tackle the still formidable problems that remain. The fight for social freedom is still inconclusive, with some battles won and some battles lost, and the issue very much in doubt. In all these struggles, this much is clear, that whatever their nature and outcome may finally prove to be, economic and social radicalism has been a powerful force in Middle Eastern affairs and has given a new drive and direction to both nationalism and religion.

4

∾∾∾∾∾∾∾∾∾

Patriotism and Nationalism

It is a universal habit of human societies to divide people into insiders and outsiders and to find opprobrious names for the latter. The two most articulate peoples of antiquity called the rest gentiles and barbarians; medieval Islam and Christendom called each other infidels; in many modern societies, the term "foreigner" combines the worst features of both barbarity and unbelief. An amended Latin tag—"I regard no alien as a human being"—might serve as the motto of a good deal of twentieth-century statesmanship and administrative practice.

In Europe and in other countries of European civilization, it has been the custom for some time past to classify people, for political purposes, by nationality. There has been some variation in the use of this term. In English (both British and American) and in French the word "nationality," or *nationalité*, indicates the country or state of which one is a citizen or subject. In German, *Staatsangehörigkeit*—state belonging—is used in this sense, while the term *Nationalität*, though etymologically akin to "nationality," is semantically different, with an ethnic rather than a legal–political sense. Soviet usage adopted and formalized this distinction. The Soviet visa form and other documents had separate rubrics for *Grazhdanstvo* (citizenship) and *Nationalnost*, which corresponds in meaning to the German *Nationalität* and not to the English or French "nationality." Apart from these formal differences of usage, different nations and parties have, from time to time, variously stressed the importance of citizenship, descent, language, religion, and other factors in determining national identity. But allowing for all these variations, it remains broadly true that in Europe and the Americas, identity and loyalty are defined in terms of nationality—that is, to varying extents, by the polity of which one is a citizen, the country one inhabits, and, in most countries in the Eastern Hemisphere, the stock from which one is deemed to descend and the language one speaks.

This has not been so in the Islamic world. Descent, language, and habitation were all of secondary importance, and it is only during the last century that under European influence, the concept of the political nation has begun to make headway. For Muslims, the basic division—the touchstone by which men are separated from one another, by which one distinguishes between brother and stranger—is that of faith, of membership in a religious community. In our day, "faith" is perhaps the wrong word. We all know—from our daily newspapers, if not from our own experience—that dislike of other religions long survives any effective belief in our own. What is meant is, rather, religion as a social and communal force, a measure of identity and a focus of group loyalty.

Within the universal Muslim community, the Muslim accepted as brothers, at least theoretically, other Muslims of whatever language, origin, or place of habitation. He rejected as aliens his own compatriots who might be of the same stock and speak the same language, but professed another religion. He also rejected his own non-Muslim ancestors, with whom he felt little or no sense of identity or continuity. The peoples of the Islamic Middle East did not neglect antiquity because they were barbarous or ignorant, incapable of understanding the importance of such things. On the contrary, they were peoples of high culture, with an unusually strong sense of history and of their place in it. But for them, real history began with the advent of Islam. Their spiritual ancestors were the early Muslims in Arabia and the heartlands; the heathen Egyptians, Babylonians, and others were remote and alien peoples with whom, despite the accidental and unimportant links of blood and soil, they had no real connection. It was only in the nineteenth century, when European archaeology revealed something of the value of this forgotten past, that they began to take an interest in it—an interest that grew and developed as it became associated with the newly imported Western ideas of the fatherland and nation, of the mystical and continuing identity of a people and the country they inhabit.

The Ottoman Empire was the last and the most enduring of the great Islamic universal empires that had ruled over the Middle East since the day when the first of the caliphs succeeded the last of the prophets. Within it, the basic loyalty of Muslims was to Islam, to the Islamic empire that was its political embodiment, and to the dynasty, legitimized by time and acceptance, that ruled over it. The discontented and the rebellious might seek a change of ministers, of sovereign—even, in a few cases, of dynasty—but they never sought to change the basis of statehood or corporate identity.

In this respect, the situation in the Middle East until the nineteenth—perhaps even the twentieth—century was not unlike that which existed in medieval Europe. The greatest poet of medieval Christendom, Dante, in his dreams of reviving a universal Christian Roman empire, was not disturbed by the fact that the Roman emperors of his day happened to be German and not Italian. Italy and the Italians existed and were of profound importance, but their true political expression was as a part of the universal Christian monarchy. The idea of Italy as a political entity, needing to express its territorial and national identity in statehood, lay far in the future. In the same way, until the impact of European political ideas, the Arab subjects of the Ottoman Empire, though well aware of their separate linguistic and cultural identity and of the historic memories attached to them, had no conception of a separate Arab state and no serious desire to part from the Turks. Certainly, they did not question the fact that the sultans happened to be Turkish. On the contrary, they would have found it odd had they been anything else. So alien was the idea of the territorial nation-state that Arabic has no word for Arabia, and Turkish, until modern times, lacked a word for Turkey. The Turks now use a word of European origin; the Arabs make do with an expression meaning the peninsula of the Arabs.

The old order continued to function more or less effectively until the introduction of new ideas from Europe began to undermine the firm basis of acceptance on which it had rested. The impact of Western action and example was changing the structure of society and the state; the influence of Western thought and practice encouraged the emergence of new political conceptions, affecting both the pattern of authority in the state and the basis of association of its subjects. During the nineteenth and twentieth centuries, the old Islamic and dynastic loyalties that prevailed among the Turks, Arabs, and Persians were modified, transformed, and, at times, replaced by the disruptive European ideas of patriotism and nationalism, with their new, abstract theories of country and nation to obscure the older realities of state and faith.

Today the three major peoples of the Middle East, the Turks, Arabs, and Persians, have become intellectually isolated from one another. Each was for long absorbed in its own dialogue with the West, and had little knowledge of the other two, or interest in them, beyond the surface movement of political events. Arabic is still taught as a classical and scriptural language in Iranian secondary schools—and conveys about as much contact with Arab movements as the vestigial teaching of Greek in English public schools does with modern Greece. Classical Arabic has also been reintroduced in Turkish religious seminaries and, at a rather elementary level, forms a part of religious instruction among Muslims generally. Apart from this, foreign Middle Eastern languages are studied in the Middle East only by small groups of students in specialist and learned institutions. The general public knows nothing of the other two languages and, until the Iranian revolution of 1979, was almost totally ignorant of the intellectual and cultural movements expressed in them. After the revolution of 1979, the new leadership in Iran made a determined effort to bring the Islamic revolution to other Muslim, and especially Arab, countries. They were able to achieve some local successes, notably among the Shīʿa population of war-torn south Lebanon. They also no doubt contributed to the establishment of an Islamic fundamentalist regime in the Sudan and to attempts to install similar regimes elsewhere. But after the elation in the first flush of revolution, their influence diminished considerably and in particular had remarkably little effect among the educated middle class or, more generally, among intellectuals. Cairo, Tehran, and Istanbul had become culturally very remote from one another. They may still look outward for guidance and inspiration, but they do not look to one another.

It was not always so. In the nineteenth century, Arabic was still read and understood by most educated Muslims; Turkish was still an imperial language, the medium of communication of the last great independent Muslim empire, to which Muslims everywhere looked as their guide and final hope. Today, a knowledge of Turkish is a rarity in the Arab lands. In Ottoman times it was a language of government and education in the cities of Syria and Iraq and survived even in Egypt, until yesterday, as a language of the court and aristocracy. Persian was the hallmark of an educated gentleman in the Ottoman lands; Ottoman Turkish was read and understood by important elements among the Turkic-speaking populations in

Transcaucasia, Iran, and Central Asia. Apart from ease of communication, the three peoples were still near to one another in spirit and outlook and had not yet grown apart into a series of separate, insulated nation-states. New ideas and new moods could still be communicated swiftly all over the Middle East, and it is only in the larger framework of the area as a whole that the separate development of the Turks, Arabs, and Persians can be adequately understood.

Turkey was the most advanced and most powerful country in the region, the most sophisticated and experienced nation, with the longest and closest acquaintance with Europe. It was natural that the new ideas should first have appeared among the Turks and have been transmitted by them to their subjects and neighbors.

"Patriotism" and "nationalism" are the words that express the normal kind of political loyalty and identity in the modern world. Both are words of unstable and therefore explosive content and so need to be handled with care. In English usage, the two convey very different suggestions and associations. Patriotism, most of us would agree, is right and good—the love and loyalty that all of us owe to our country. Nationalism, on the other hand, is something rather alien and therefore rather suspect. The expression "English nationalism," for example, does not come very naturally to the tongue. One thinks of nationalism as being Celtic or continental, African or Oriental, but not English and not American.

The first stirrings of the new loyalty in the Middle East took the form of patriotism, not nationalism. They were inspired by the example of Western Europe, particularly of France and England, where nationhood and statehood were combined and where patriotism was the loyalty that citizens owed to their country and normally paid to the government when it fell due. This new conception, which seemed to reinforce and extend the claims of the state to the loyalty of its subjects, at first received some encouragement from Middle Eastern governments; later they found that the transfer of allegiance from a person to an abstraction raised unexpected difficulties.

The term used to convey the idea of country, or more precisely of the French *patrie,* was the Arab word *waṭan,* which has passed, with some changes of pronunciation, into Persian, Turkish, and other Islamic languages. The primary meaning of *waṭan* was a person's place of origin or habitation, usually used of a town, village, or at most a province. A person's *waṭan* could be the object of sentiment, affection, and devotion, as many passages in classical

Islamic literature attest, and is associated with family affection, memories of youth, and home-sickness. From these it is clear that the classical word *waṭan* was the equivalent not of the French *patrie*, but, rather, of the English word "home" in its broader sense. Like "home," it carried a wealth of sentimental associations, notably in the period of the Crusades when so many homes were lost or threatened; like it again, it had no political content.

The use of the word *waṭan* (Turkish, *vatan*) in a political sense, equivalent to the French *patrie* or the English "country" or the German *Vaterland*, dates from the late eighteenth century and is clearly due to European influence and example. The earliest occurrence that I have been able to trace in this sense is in a Turkish document, a report by Morali Esseyyid Ali Efendi, who served as Ottoman ambassador in Paris under the Directoire. In a description of the hospitals and homes provided by the French authorities for pensioned and disabled soldiers, he speaks of these men as having striven "in the cause of the Republic [*jumhur*] and out of zeal for the country [*vatan*]."[1] Both words, *jumhur* and *vatan*, were old, with roots in classical Arabic. *Jumhur* had already acquired a political connotation at an earlier date, through Ottoman acquaintance with Venice and other European republics. Patriotism was a new discovery, made known through the French Revolution, and it is doubtful whether Ali Efendi, whose reports do not suggest any great keenness of perception, really understood it. More probably, he, or rather his interpreter, was merely translating literally from a French original, without appreciating its real import.

Nevertheless, the new idea spread, and in 1839 the phrase "love of country" (*vatan*) even appears in an Ottoman official document, the famous reform edict known as the Rescript of the Rosebower. In 1840 the Turkish diplomat Mustafa Sami, in his *Essay on Europe*, speaks of "love of country" as one of the praiseworthy qualities of the people of Paris and adduces his own love of country as his reason for publishing this booklet. By 1841 the expression *hubb ül-vatan*, (love of country) was sufficiently established in its new meaning to appear as the equivalent of patriotism in Handjeri's Turkish–French dictionary, where it is illustrated with a number of phrases expressing patriotic sentiments. In 1851 the Turkish poet and journalist Shinasi, in a letter to his mother, said, "I want to sacrifice myself for my religion, state, country and nation" (*din ve devlet ve vatan ve millet*). The Crimean War was the occasion for a more militant patriotism and the appearance of the first patriotic poem. By this time the word *vatan* was in current journalistic usage; in 1866 it even appeared in the name of a new newspaper, the *Ayine-i Vatan* (Mirror of the Fatherland).[2]

The appearance of patriotic ideas in Egypt came a little later than in Turkey and was to a large extent the work of Sheikh Rifāʿā Rāfiʿ al-Ṭahṭāwī. During his stay in Paris from 1826 to 1831, he must have become aware of the significance of patriotism in French life, though he makes little reference to it in his book on France. His patriotic writings came some years later and enjoyed official encouragement. In 1855 he published an "Egyptian patriotic ode" (*qaṣīda waṭaniyya Miṣriyya*) in praise of the new ruler Saʿīd Pasha and, in the same year, a collection of "Egyptian patriotic poems" (*manẓūmāt waṭaniyya Miṣriyya*), inspired by the exploits of the Egyptian contingent sent to help the Turks in the Crimean War. Another patriotic ode greeted the accession of Ismāʿīl eight years later, and further *waṭaniyyāt* (patriotic poems) appeared in 1868 after the return of the Egyptian, actually black, battalion from Mexico, where they had gone as part of Napoleon III's expeditionary force.

Sheikh Rifāʿa's patriotic poems, some of them in simple, martial verse, sing the praises of Egypt, of the Egyptian soldier and army, and of the khedivial dynasty. In his prose works, he develops his patriotic teachings at greater length, citing the tradition that "love of country is part of the faith" and other dicta. Patriotism, for Sheikh Rifāʿa, is the bond that holds the social order together; to inculcate it in the young is one of the primary purposes of education. His patriotism is clearly and distinctively Egyptian. It is not Arab, since it does not include the other Arabic-speaking or Muslim countries, and since it *does* include the ancient Egyptians of pre-Islamic times and even the non-Muslim residents of Egypt in his own day. As far back as 1838, Sheikh Rifāʿa had produced the first Arabic translation of a European history of pharaonic Egypt. In 1868 he tried his own hand at a history of Egypt from antiquity up to the Arab conquest, thus ending where all previous Arabic histories of Egypt had begun. His later works are full of a sentiment of pride in the glories of ancient Egypt and of a deep love for his country, which he sees as a living, continuing entity from the days of the pharaohs to his own. This was a new and radical idea in the Muslim world, and it was long before its equivalent appeared in any other Muslim country.

Sheikh Rifāʿa's brand of patriotism was sponsored and encouraged by the khedives, who saw, in the emergence of a distinctively Egyptian political personality and loyalty, a support for their own dynastic and separatist ambitions. Members of the khedivial family also helped, for different reasons, to launch another brand of patriotism, that of the Turkish group of liberal patriots known as the Young Ottomans.

The 1850s and 1860s brought important developments. The war had aroused a passionate desire for news and interpretation; the telegraph and the press came to supply them. The strains of the Crimean War and the example of Turkey's Western allies stimulated the growth of patriotism, which found expression in the new and widely read newspaper and magazine press. The Young Ottoman group, formed in 1865 to press for a more liberal political regime in the empire, based themselves from the start on a patriotic as well as a liberal program.

Namık Kemal, the intellectual leader of the group, wrote eloquently in both prose and verse on patriotism—on the greatness of his country and the loyalty owed to it by its citizens. The first leader of the first issue of *Hürriyet* (Freedom), the journal published by the exiled liberals in London in 1868, is headed *Ḥubb al-waṭan min al-īmān* (Love of country is part of the faith), a tradition now becoming popular among the new patriots. The same theme is argued and developed in a series of articles, published both during his stay in Europe and after his return to Turkey in 1870. Kemal went into exile again in 1873, following the too enthusiastic reception of his ardently patriotic play *Vatan or Silistre*, celebrating an episode in the Crimean War.

The unit of Namık Kemal's patriotism is the Ottoman Empire—its sovereign, its territory, its peoples. The word "Turk" appears rarely in his writings and then as a synonym of Ottoman Muslim. The word "Ottoman," as used by him and his contemporaries, is often limited to Muslims, but at other times refers to all the sultan's subjects irrespective of religion or race, who are to be united in a single loyalty. Kemal's conceptions of nation and country are confused, often contradictory, and change during the course of his career. They are overshadowed by his constant loyalty to his religion. Despite his use of the terms "country" and "patriot" and his appeals to his non-Muslim fellow citizens, the entity that he serves is ultimately Islamic. This can be seen most clearly in his many historical writings and allusions. He is uninterested in the history of Turkey before the coming of the Muslim Turks; he is equally uninterested in the history of the Turks before their conversion to Islam. Kemal's *Vatan* had been ruled in the past by Arab caliphs as well as Turkish sultans, and its sons include Arab and Persian sages as well as Turkish heroes. There is nothing in Kemal's patriotism to resemble the clear sense of identity and continuity of Egypt and the Egyptians expressed in the writings of Sheikh Rifā'a. Kemal was a critic and not a spokesman of the regime, a journalist more than a teacher, but still a member of the ruling group of an empire. The inconsistencies of his ideas are perhaps a measure of their relevance and their reality, in an age of great changes still imperfectly understood.

In several of his essays, Kemal offers his readers reassurance against the dangers of separatism among the many peoples and races of the empire. It is true, he says, that the population of the empire is very diverse. The different peoples are, however, so thoroughly mixed that none of them is strong enough in any region to form a viable separate state or to join an existing one. The only exception is the Arab provinces, which are inhabited by a people of many millions, speaking another language and feeling themselves to belong to another race. They were, however, Muslims, "bound to us by Islamic brotherhood and allegiance to the Caliphate"[3] and would not therefore break away in the name of Arabism or the like.

Kemal was wrong on both points, although the proof of his errors lay far in the future. For the time being, the Arab provinces did indeed remain bound by Islamic brotherhood and dynastic loyalty, which meant far more to them than the newfangled notion of Ottoman patriotism. An exception was the Christian Arab elite of Beirut and Lebanon, where patriotic ideas evoked a certain response. As Christians, they were more open to European ideas. But unlike the Armenian and Greek-speaking Christians of Anatolia and Rumelia, they shared the language and culture of their Muslim neighbors and had no memories of separate national identity. On several occasions, most recently in 1860, they had suffered severely from religious persecution. They therefore had every inducement to favor a patriotic instead of a religious basis of allegiance. If language, culture, domicile, and citizenship were to be the criteria of identity, then the Christian Arabs might hope that their possession of the first three would entitle them to the fourth and would give them the unrestricted, first-class membership that they lacked in the Islamic empire. As early as 1860 Buṭrus al-Bustānī founded a school called al-Madrasa al-waṭaniyya and addressed his appeals for solidarity and loyalty to his Muslim and Christian compatriots. In 1870 he used the formula "love of country is part of the faith" as the motto of his fortnightly magazine *Al-Jinān*. Bustānī writes as a loyal Ottoman subject, but the *waṭan* of which he speaks is Syria, a province of the empire rather than the whole of it. Some Maronite Christians, angered by Muslim persecution and sustained by memories of Lebanese autonomy, even thought of an anti-Ottoman Lebanese patriotism, similar to the movements of the Greeks and Serbs. These were the only stirrings of disloyalty at that time in the Arab provinces, which otherwise remained faithful to the Islamic Ottaman Empire.

Egypt, then, was the only country where territorial, nonconfessional patriotism made any headway among a Muslim people. There were many advantages: a country strikingly defined by both history and geography, a vigorous reigning dynasty determined to achieve territorial independence, and a splendid ancient past—the first to be rediscovered and in many ways the most magnificent—to sustain patriotic pride. In 1882 a new and powerful stimulus to patriotic feeling was provided—the British occupation. Even before the coming of the British, the growing feeling against foreigners had found expression in the famous slogan "Egypt for the Egyptians," launched by the Christian journalist Selīm Naqqāsh, popularized by the Jewish pamphleteer Abū Naddāra, and applied by the Muslim soldier ʿUrābī Pasha. During the 1870s, several developments in Egypt had led to mounting resentment and improved ways of expressing it. On the one hand, there were a shallow Nile, a weak and spendthrift government, and growing foreign influence; on the other, an expanding newspaper press, improved education, and an influx of writers and intellectuals from the unfree lands of Islamic Asia—notably the pan-Islamic leader Jamāl al-Dīn al-Afghānī and a number of journalists, mostly Christian, from Ottoman Syria. In 1879 a group of Egyptians formed al-ḥizb al-waṭanī, usually translated as the National party, though Patriotic party would be a more literal rendering. This was followed, after the British occupation, by a series of other societies, associations, and parties, expressing, in various degrees and in different ways, opposition to foreign rule. The most important was the National party led by Muṣṭafā Kāmil, the political and intellectual leader of Egyptian resistance at the end of the nineteenth and the beginning of the twentieth century.

It would be a mistake to regard these as purely patriotic national liberation movements. The element of Muslim identity and loyalty was still very strong; it was nourished by the contemporary current of Islamic modernism and revival and sometimes found an outlet in expressions of hostility and mistrust toward non-Muslims. The resistance movements were, however, essentially Egyptian and concerned with the pursuit of Egyptian objectives. They were not anti-imperialist, merely anti-British, since Britain was the occupying power in Egypt. Muṣṭafā Kāmil's pro-French attitude was in no way affected by French action in North Africa, just as, earlier in the century, Sheikh Rifāʿa had been unconcerned with the French conquest of Algeria, which began while he was still in Paris. They were not Arab nationalists either. For Muṣṭafā Kāmil and his contemporaries, the greatness of the medieval caliphate was something in which their ancestors participated and in which they might claim a share of pride. It was, however, a dead classical past, much less vivid to them than the newly rediscovered glories of pharaonic Egypt. The Arabs of Asia were foreigners, cousins rather than brothers, and Egyptian writers like ʿAbdallah Nadīm and Muṣṭafā Kāmil at times attacked the Syrians settled in Egypt, whom they called *dukhalā'* (intruders). Insofar as their cause was part of a larger one, it was still that of Islam. ʿUrābī's movement had been directed not so much against foreigners as against the Turco-Circassian elements that dominated the army, the aristocracy, and the court. Under the British occupation, this cleavage seemed less important. Muṣṭafā Kāmil, criticizing the ʿUrābists, accused them of "ethnic hostility" and argued that the Turks and Circassians, long established in Egypt, must be regarded as Egyptianized and as part of the nation.

Even in Egypt, the Western European type of patriotism had only a limited appeal and was much modified by the impact of older and deeper loyalties. It had still less appeal in Iran and the Ottoman Empire, which were ruled by established dynasties upheld by traditional Islamic loyalty. Iran was a country inhabited by a nation with a long and distinguished history, marked off from its neighbors by its language and its Shīʿite religion. Yet despite the beginnings of a patriotic movement in literature and a nascent interest in the glories of ancient Iran, the majority of Persians seem to have retained a primarily Islamic—albeit Shīʿite—identity and loyalty and spoke of their country as the "lands of Islam." Amid the mixed population of the Ottoman Empire, patriotism—that is, Ottoman patriotism— had even less chance of success. All over the Middle East, the essential prerequisites of the Western European type of state and loyalty were lacking. There was nothing like the legal and territorial nationality of Great Britain and Switzerland, with their long traditions of ordered liberty and common identity; nothing like the political and centralist patriotism of France, resting on an ancient identity of statehood, country, language, and culture, and infused from the time of the Revolution with new and passionate libertarian ideals. Amid the ethnic confusion, political quietism, and religious collectivism of the Middle East, there seemed little prospect of their emerging.

The ever-fertile continent of Europe had, however, more than one example to offer to its neophytes and disciples elsewhere. In central and eastern Europe in the first half of the nineteenth century, there were no well-defined and old established nation-states like England, France, or Spain. Instead, there were nations and peoples lost in polyglot dynastic empires, divided into small principalities, or subject to alien rule. There were Germans, but no Germany; Poles, but no Poland; Italians, but no Italy; Hungarians, but only a shadow of Hungary. To these peoples, patriotism of the Western European type had little appeal, for it could only bind them to dynastic or foreign masters and perpetuate divisions that were becoming unacceptable. Their deepest loyalty was given not to state or country, but to the nation or people, and was expressed not in patriotism, but in nationalism. The point was made with characteristic vigor and clarity by L. B. Namier:

> Here it was not the state that moulded nationality, but a pre-existent nationality which postulated a State. The German concept of nationality is linguistic and "racial," rather than political and territorial.... The highest forms of communal life became the basis of West European nationalisms, the myth of the barbaric horde that of German nationalism.[4]

"The myth of the barbaric horde" is a vivid phrase that can be expressed in Arabic in one word, *qawmiyya*.

This kind of nationalism was concerned first with independence, unity, and power and only secondarily, if at all, with individual freedom. "One reason for dissatisfaction," wrote Prince Chlodwig zu Hohenlohe-Schillingsfürst in 1847,

> is the nullity of Germany vis-à-vis of other states.... It is sad and humiliating not to be able to say proudly abroad: "I am a German" ... but to have to say: "I am a Kurhesse, Darmstädter, Bückeburger; my Fatherland was once a great powerful country, but is now split into thirty-eight fragments."

Most supporters of pan-Arabism would have recognized and shared the feeling that inspired this remark; most of them would probably also have been willing to endorse the saying of the German liberal leader Bassermann in 1849: "If I knew the unity and future greatness of Germany were to be attained through a temporary renunciation of all the freedoms, I should be the first to submit to such a dictatorship."[5]

This kind of nationalism—romantic, subjective, often illiberal and chauvinistic, contemptuous of legal loyalties, and neglectful of personal freedom—corresponded much more closely to conditions in the collapsing polities of the Middle East. It also appealed to much older and deeper instincts of tribal identity, loyalty, and pride. In time, the new ethnic nationalism awoke an overwhelming response among its peoples. As in the countries of its origin, it has aroused passionate loyalties and evoked great efforts and achievements. But it has also again led to the loss—one might even say to the abandonment and renunciation—of political freedom.

The new ethnic nationalism came from central and eastern Europe, through several channels. The first carriers were probably the Hungarian and Polish refugees who went to Turkey after the unsuccessful revolution of 1848. Several of them stayed permanently, embraced Islam, and held important posts in the Ottoman service. One of them was Count Constantine Borzęcki, later Mustafa Jelâleddin Pasha, who in 1869 published a book in Istanbul, in French, called *Les Turcs anciens et modernes*. The main part of the book consists of a report and recommendations to the sultan on the current problems of the empire. There is also a historical section, including a survey, based on European orientalist publications, of the earlier history of the Turkic peoples, in which great stress is laid on their positive and creative role. Borzęcki is at pains to prove that the Turks are a white race, akin to the peoples of Europe and belonging to what he calls the "Touro-Aryan" race.

Count Borzęcki's transposition of Polish nationalism into a Turkish mode was supported by themes borrowed from the works of European Turcology. Some knowledge of the findings of this branch of orientalist scholarship was reaching the Turks through various channels, with significant effects on their conception of their national identity and place in history. The Turks, even more than the Persians or Arabs, had forgotten their pre-Islamic past and had sunk their identity in Islam. The Turcologists—accidentally and incidentally, for the most part—helped restore it to them and launch a new movement, which later came to be known as pan-Turkism. Its main strength was at first not among the Turks of Turkey but among the Turkic subject peoples of the Russian Empire loosely, collectively, and inaccurately called Tatars. In their attitudes toward Russia, they had gone through much the same phases and moods as had the Muslims in India and Egypt toward Britain—sullen withdrawal, response and reform, reaction and rejection. In the schools and universities of Russia, Tatar intellectuals had studied the ancient history and literature of their people and had acquired a sense of pride and identity; they had also encountered the mystical pan-

Slav nationalism of their masters and reacted against it with a pan-Turkism of their own.

Tatar exiles and émigrés from the Russian Empire brought these ideas to Turkey. At first they encountered a cool reception among the Ottoman Turks, who saw no reason to adopt a doctrine that would disrupt the multinational empire over which they ruled. The great Turkish poet Mehmet Akif was especially vehement against ethnic nationalism, which he saw as fundamentally unpatriotic and irreligious. But times were changing. The loss of province after province in Ottoman Europe to independent national states reduced the scope and indeed the purpose of Ottomanism; the departure of the non-Turkish peoples increased the relative and absolute importance of the Anatolian Turkish core of the empire that remained. The idea began to gain favor of seeking a new base of identity, not the crumbling, polyglot empire of the Ottomans, but a new unity based on the mighty and multitudinous Turkish peoples stretching from the Aegean across Asia to the China Sea.

These ideas were suppressed under Abdülhamid. They burst into the open after the revolution of 1908 and began to acquire considerable support among the Young Turks. Like the Egyptians, the Turks began to seek sustenance in their past, but it was the past of the Turks, not of Turkey, that interested them. The bounds of historical inquiry were pushed back beyond the Islamization of the Turks to the ancient history of the Turkic peoples in their Central and East Asian homelands. There was still no interest in the pre-Turkish history of Turkey—in Byzantium or Troy or the ancient states of Asia Minor. This did not come until a generation later.

Turkism is thus a form of nationalism, not of patriotism. The focus of loyalty was not the amorphous Ottoman Empire or the effete Ottoman state, but the vigorous Turkish family of nations, most of whom lived beyond the frontiers of Turkey, "the last independent fragment of the Turkish world," as a pan-Turkist once called it. In 1914 Turkey found itself at war with two great allies against Russia, the imperial power that ruled over most of the Turkic lands and peoples. For the first time, there seemed a serious possibility of achieving the pan-Turkish dream. In the words of the poet-sociologist Ziya Gökalp,

> The land of the enemy shall be devastated
> Turkey shall be enlarged and become Turan.[6]

After a period of discouragement caused by the defeats of the Ottoman armies in the field, hope flared again after 1917, when the outbreak of revolution and civil war in Russia and the collapse of Russian authority in Central Asia and Transcaucasia seemed to bring the moment of Turkic liberation and unity very near. The leaders of the Turkish republic, which emerged from the ruins of the Ottoman Empire, avoided such entanglements and discouraged such ambitions, preferring instead to concentrate on the immense task of rebuilding their ruined homeland. During the Second World War, there was a brief revival of pan-Turkish propaganda. It was due in the main to Nazi instigation and encouragement and was intended as a weapon in the German war against the Soviet Union. But apart from a few radical right-wing intellectuals, it won little support and disappeared after the defeat of Nazi Germany. The breakup of the Soviet Union and the emergence of five independent Turkic republics reopened the issue, and offered new challenges to the one Turkish state that had never lost its independence and was seen by many as a model of modernization and democracy.

Some Egyptians showed an increasing interest in the idea of representative government for the nation, which was still further stimulated by the Persian and Turkish constitutional revolutions. The Organic and Electoral Laws of 1913 and the Constitution of 1923 were stages in the development of such a program. Their loyalty was to Egypt, patriotic rather than nationalist. They took pride in their Arabic language and culture and in their Islamic religion, but rejected both Arabism and Islamism as the focus of identity and loyalty. For the Arabs of Asia—those of them who had not settled in Egypt—they felt a sympathetic interest based on historical and cultural links, but no common political bond. Their attitude might be described as corresponding roughly to that of an American toward England or, better still, that of a Mexican, proud and conscious of his Aztec past, toward Spain. Muṣṭafā Kāmil even condemned the first stirrings of pan-Arabism as a British plot aimed against the Ottoman Empire and caliphate.

This kind of secular, liberal patriotism drew its leaders and spokesmen chiefly from the new professional and semiprofessional class of lawyers, officials, teachers, and journalists. Because of both their education and their function, they were the least traditional and most Westernized of all elements in Egyptian society. For this very reason, they remained isolated from the majority of the Egyptian people, for whose resentments they provided, for a while, an outlet and an instrument, but for whom their aspirations and their ideologies were alien and meaningless. Their failure, disastrous and final, came when their program of national sovereignty and constitutional government was fulfilled, thus revealing its irrelevance to Egyptian facts and its insufficiency for Egyptian needs. Liberal, secular patriotism languished and died during the bitter struggles of the 1940s. Its corpse was incinerated on 26 January 1952—Black Saturday, when the mob burned the center of Cairo and destroyed some buildings, a society, and a regime. Among the claimants to the inheritance at that time, two predominated: the new pan-Islamism of the Muslim Brotherhood, and the ethnic and communal nationalism of the pan-Arabs, which was spreading from Asia.

Some of the more exuberant exponents of modern Arab nationalism have at various times traced its origins back to Muḥammad ʿAlī, to Saladin, to the caliph ʿUmar, and to Hammurabi king of Akkad. Without attaching too much importance to such flights of fancy, it must be said that the Arab sense of separate identity is very old and deeply rooted. In pre-Islamic and early Islamic times, the Arabs had a strong ethnic and aristocratic feeling, which, in the cosmopolitan Islamic empire, gave way to a kind of cultural self-awareness based on the common possession of the sacred and scriptural Arabic language. As the philologist al-Thaʿālibī (d. 1038) put it:

> Whoever loves the Prophet loves the Arabs, and whoever loves the Arabs loves the Arabic language in which the best of books was revealed ... whomsoever God has guided to Islam ... believes that Muḥammad is the best of Prophets ... that the Arabs are the best of peoples ... and that Arabic is the best of languages.[7]

The justified pride of the Arabs in their magnificent language and in the rich and splendid literature it enshrines found frequent expression over the centuries. Arabism as a *political* movement, however—as a belief that the speakers of Arabic form a nation with national rights and aspirations—dates only from the late nineteenth century, and it was for long confined to small and unrepresentative groups, most of them Christian. The overwhelming majority of Arabs remained faithful to the Ottoman Empire until it was destroyed. The Arabs were Muslim subjects of a Muslim empire. A popular, national movement such as those that impelled the Christian Serbs and Greeks to revolution and liberty did not and could not arise among them. The small groups of intellectuals who preached an Arab renascence found little response; even the British-sponsored revolt in Arabia was neither as successful in its appeal nor as wholehearted in its purposes as the official legend suggests.

There were some individuals, however, more significant for the future than for their own contemporaries, who had begun to think in terms of an Arab national revival. Just as pan-Slavism in the Russian Empire had evoked a pan-Turkish response among the Turkic subject peoples, so pan-Turkism, transplanted from the Russian to the Ottoman Empire, helped arouse an Arab national feeling among those Ottomans who were Muslim but not Turkish. Political Arabism was born about the turn of the century and was fostered chiefly by Syrians, especially by Syrian emigrants to khedivial Egypt such as ʿAbd al-Raḥmān al-Kawākibī (1849–1902) and Muḥammad Rashīd Riḍā (1865–1935). The former appears to have been first to come out openly against the Turks and the Ottoman sultan and to demand an Arab state with an Arab caliph.

After 1918, Arab resentment was directed against less ambiguous and more rewarding enemies—not the Turks and their caliph, but imperialism and Zionism, easily identified with such older and more familiar entities as the Christians and the Jews. Deprived of their old religious and dynastic loyalties, living in artificial political units created by the conquerors, subject to the rule of alien and infidel masters, the Arabs could find little satisfaction in patriotism and at that time showed little interest in liberalism or socialism of the kind that flourished in India and Southeast Asia. Instead, they turned to an ethnic nationalism of central European type, which in the 1930s drew new inspiration from the central European fountainhead. At first, the Egyptians stood aloof from this movement and were taunted with their "pharaonism." Under the military regime, the Egyptians, too, threw in their lot with Arabism, so thoroughly that the very name of Egypt was for a while wiped off the map, a result that none of the many foreign invaders and oppressors of Egypt had ever been able to achieve.

The word used to express the notion of ethnic nationalism is *qawmiyya*, an abstract noun formed from *qawm*, meaning, in classical Arabic, people, followers, group, or tribe, especially the group of kinsfolk mobilized for mutual support. It is in this last sense that the word is used of the North African tribal levies called *goum*, a dialectal pronunciation of the same word. Like *waṭan*, *qawmiyya* is of Arabic etymology, but was first used in its modern political sense in Turkish, the first Muslim language to require and coin new words for new, Western ideas. In its Turkish form, *kavmiyet*, the word occurs in the writings of the Young Ottomans as a term for ethnic and local—literally, tribal—nationalities or nationalisms, which conflict with the larger loyalties of the Ottoman sultanate and Islam. Thus in 1870, Ali Suavi criticized a muddleheaded semiofficial Ottoman proposal that the Sublime Porte should, like Italy and Prussia, take up the cause of nationality (kavmiyet) and unite all the Muslims. Ali Suavi rightly pointed out that nationality in Europe meant something entirely different: "Among us there is no problem of nationality. Problems of nationality would cause our ruin. The unification of the Muslims could at most be a question of religion, not a question of nationality."[8] Two years later, Namık Kemal wrote an eloquent plea for harmony and unity between the different peoples (kavim) making up the Ottoman Empire, in a common patriotism to their Ottoman vatan. He insisted that race and religion were secondary to the major facts of country and citizenship and could best be safeguarded by loyalty to the liberal and tolerant Ottoman state, rather than by breaking it into squabbling and non-viable ethnic fragments.[9]

Namık Kemal was, of course, concerned chiefly about the Christian Balkan peoples and not about the Turks themselves, who were still far from thinking in ethnic or national terms. His appeal was in vain. Nationalism spread rapidly among the Ottoman Christians and was communicated by them to the Muslims—Albanians, Arabs, and even the Turks themselves. The Albanian national rising in 1912 provoked a passionate rejection from the Muslim patriot, antinationalist poet Mehmet Akif, himself of Albanian extraction:

> Your nationality [milliyet] was Islam ... what is this
>   tribalism [kavmiyet]?
> Is the Arab any better than the Turk, the Laz than the
>   Cherkes or the Kurd,
> The Persian than the Chinese? In what?
> Could Islam be broken up into component parts? What
>   is happening?
> The Prophet himself cursed the idea of tribalism!
>
> The Turk cannot live without the Arab. Who says he can,
>   is mad.
> For the Arab, the Turk is his right eye and his right hand.
>
> Let the Albanians be a warning to you
> What confused policy is this, what evil cause?
>
> Hear this from me, who am myself an Albanian....
> I say no more—alas my afflicted country ...[10]

Mehmet Akif was fighting a lost cause. He realized this himself when after a brief association with the Kemalists in Anatolia, during which he wrote the poem that became the national anthem of the Turkish republic, he withdrew to voluntary exile in Cairo. The cause of nationalism spread, ultimately involving all the peoples of the Middle East.

In Iran, a country defined by language, territory, and statehood, the identification of nationalism with a kind of Muslim patriotism was fairly easy. The Iranians are devoutly Islamic, but they are also Shī'ite and thus marked off from almost all their neighbors. The former Soviet Azerbaijan is also Shī'ite, but is a lost province of Iran. Iraq has a Shī'ite majority, but for centuries has been subject to Sunni domination. The historic personality of the modern Iranian state, founded by the Safavid dynasty at the beginning of the sixteenth century, has been shaped by its self-perception as a bastion of Shī'a Islam surrounded by hostile Sunni powers based in the Ottoman lands, in Central Asia, and in India.

Iran is also divided from its neighbors by language. Apart from Tadjikistan and Afghanistan, where a form of Persian known as Dari is one of the country's two official languages, Iran is surrounded by speakers of Arabic and a number of Turkic and Indic languages. And even the Afghans and Tadjiks are mostly Sunni.

In these circumstances, it was natural that a strong sense of identity and loyalty should develop based on the Shī'ite faith, the Persian language and culture, and the ancient and historic land of Iran. The relative importance of these and the competing claims of communalism, nationalism, and patriotism have formed a major theme of Iranian debate in this century. The theme of patriotism, of identity based on the land of Iran, has received considerable encouragement in recent decades from the restoration of ancient monuments, the recovery and translation of long-forgotten ancient texts, and the addition of a new dimension to Persian pride and self-awareness. This was encouraged as a matter of policy by the late shah, who, while not entirely neglecting the religious aspect, tried to inculcate in his people a sense of Iranian destiny, of an enduring, unchanging Iran surviving through successive changes of religion and culture and reasserting itself after each foreign invasion. In the shah's version of patriotism, the centralizing and leading role of the monarchy naturally occupied a position of some importance.

In this perspective, the Arab Islamic invasion of the seventh century was not fundamentally different from the earlier conquest by Alexander or the later conquest by the Mongols: the imposition of an alien domination and culture. This was, of course, anathema to religious fundamentalists, who saw in the Islamic conquest the providential opening of Iran to the true faith and who denounced the cult of antiquity as a return to paganism.

In the Soviet Middle East, nationalism had a more checkered career. After the Russian Revolution, national regimes of various political complexions appeared in Central Asia and Transcaucasia. These all were overcome by the Red Army, and the authority of Moscow was restored. Thereafter, nationalism of all forms was considered an offense. From time to time, reports appeared that such offenders had been detected and punished. The most striking case occurred in 1938, when Feyzullah Khojayev, first minister of the Uzbek Republic, and Akmal Ikramov, secretary-general of the Uzbek Communist party, were charged as nationalists and British spies and were shot. This association of offenses, which may seem strange farther south, was for long commonplace in the Soviet Middle East. Soviet spokesmen and their local protégés devoted considerable energy to denouncing the three cardinal errors of pan-Turkism, pan-Iranism, and pan-Islamism. The first would have linked the Turkic-speaking republics with one another and with Turkey; the second would have created a bond between Persian speakers in Tadjikistan and those in Afghanistan and Iran; the third, and in Soviet eyes the most dangerous, would have linked all the Muslim peoples of the Soviet Union with the great world of Islam beyond the frontier and opened them to dangerous and uncontrollable influences. The weakening of Soviet central power and the effective breakup of the Soviet Union in 1991 gave free play to these influences, and the six republics with Muslim majorities now face major choices.

Another brand of nationalism, strikingly different from the Muslim nationalisms in some respects but surprisingly similar in others, is Jewish nationalism, one of the elements contributing to the growth of political Zionism. The corporate self-awareness of the Jews, like that of the Arabs, is as old as their corporate existence. Like that of the Arabs, it passed through tribal, ethnic, and cultural phases to achieve its most characteristic and most enduring form in religion.

Jewish nationalism began in central and eastern Europe, where the unemancipated, unassimilated Jewish communities formed an entity with all the current criteria of nationhood but two—the possession of a national language and the occupation of a national territory. The Hebrew renascence and the Zionist movement aimed at supplying these two deficiencies. Some substitutes were suggested; the east European Jews did in fact have a language of their own—an archaic Franconian dialect, now known as Yiddish—which they had retained after their medieval migration from the Germanic to the Slavonic lands and which had developed into a rich and flexible language with a remarkable literature. For a while, a kind of Yiddish cultural nationalism found some support, particularly on the left, for the idea of a Jewish secular and popular culture based on the language of the masses. This program, like the so-called Territorialist movement, which accepted the idea of a national home but wanted to have it in some place more convenient and less troublesome than Palestine, failed to win support among the Jewish masses, to whom their ideas seemed pointless and irrelevant. In the early nineteenth century, the nationalist fervor of the Germans, Hungarians, and Poles also involved their Jewish minorities, many of whom felt, fought, and died as Germans, Hungarians, and Poles, for the German, Hungarian, or Polish cause. But the ethnic and often chauvinistic nationalism of these peoples made it difficult for them to accept the Jews as part of the nation, and during the late nineteenth century a sharp cleavage appeared among secularized and national-minded Jews in central and eastern Europe, between those who continued the struggle for acceptance in the reluctant nation and those who turned away to the idea of a separate Jewish nation in its own homeland—the idea, in a word, of Zionism. For traditional religious Jews, nationalism of any kind was an impiety. For the Jews of the democratic West, the question hardly arose, and Zionism was, or seemed to be, largely a philanthropic matter. In central and eastern Europe, the modernized Jews, faced with an intolerable situation, were offered a choice between two solutions: assimiliation into the nation as individuals or assimilation into nationhood as a community. The rise of militant anti-Semitism removed the first choice and vastly increased the range and force of the Zionist appeal.

The physical destruction of most of the Jews of continental Europe by the Nazis and their accomplices, and the limited choices available to the survivors, generated a powerful, and in the event irresistible, movement for the creation of a Jewish homeland and a Jewish state. The Christian world, moved by feelings of guilt and compassion, offered little resistance and some support. The Palestinians and their allies, discredited in Western eyes by their wartime record of sympathy for the Axis and hostility to the Allies, failed, first politically and then militarily, in their attempts to prevent the establishment of this state. The attempt and its failure had tragic consequences for the Palestinian people.

Israel

In the brutal aftermath of the Second World War and amid the liquidation of old empires and the creation of a new one, some old frontiers were redrawn, some new ones were created, and many millions of people fled or were driven from their homes in eastern Europe, Asia, and Africa. The problem of the Palestinian refugees was by no means the largest of these, but it proved the most enduring and the most bitter. The success of the Palestinians in preserving their identity is even more remarkable in that Palestine as a separate political entity known by that name lasted for only thirty years, from the establishment to the end of the British mandate, and the refugees for the most part lived among peoples of the same language, religion, and culture. In all Arab countries except Jordan, citizenship was refused to Palestinian refugees. Their descendants, even to the third and fourth generations, remained aliens, deprived of political rights and liable to expulsion. All this further embittered the already difficult problem of relations between the new Jewish state and its Arab neighbors, and for a long time a solution seemed beyond the range of possibility.

In 1948 and 1949, the newborn Jewish state narrowly survived its first ordeal by battle. Several more Arab–Israeli wars were fought before the first major step was taken toward peace, with the signature of the Israeli–Egyptian peace treaty in 1979, more than thirty years after the foundation of the state. In the meantime, despite the anomalies of its external relations, Israel was becoming internally more and more like a normal country, and Zionism, at least for its citizens, was gradually being transformed into an Israeli patriotism.

But even today, in the modern, national state of Israel, the Jew may be an agnostic or even an atheist and still pass muster. But let him adopt another religion, and he ceases to be a Jew in any sense that is acceptable to the state, the law, and the overwhelming majority of the people. It may be that, given time, Israel will develop into an ordinary secular nation—it has not done so yet. Perhaps the nearest analogy—although the differences are great and obvious—is Pakistan, where the attempt is also being made, after struggle, upheaval, and partition, to form a new, modern nation based on a religious community.

We have traced the rise and fall of liberal patriotism, the rise and spread of ethnic nationalism. It remains to glance briefly at the most recent phase: the return, at first tentative and uncertain and then increasingly vigorous, to a new patriotism based on new nation-states that are at last beginning to take root in the consciousness and loyalties of their peoples.

The process began with and has gone furthest among the Turks. In 1922, in the moment of victory over the Greeks, they still faced great uncertainties. They were, to borrow a phrase, a people who had lost an empire and not yet found a new role in the world. In the struggle for national liberation, many themes occur—Islam and pan-Islam, Turkism and pan-Turkism, and hostility to the imperialist West. The theme of Turkey—of the fatherland of a nation called the Turks—was for long a comparatively minor one. Yet the form of the struggle, which was to eject foreign invaders from the redefined national territory, inevitably gave it the character of a patriotic war and prepared the way for a new patriotism based on an entity hitherto unknown to Turks—the state and land of Turkey. Resisting the temptations offered by the upheaval in Russia, Mustafa Kemal (later surnamed Atatürk) renounced all pan-Islamic and pan-Turkish aims and ambitions and persuaded his people to do the same. Turkish and Muslim brothers in other lands must fight their own battles; the Turks had urgent and difficult tasks to perform in their own country. Alone among the peoples of the Middle East, the Turks could claim no readily identifiable ancestors in the area in antiquity. Atatürk gave them the Trojans and the Hittites and, through the intensive cultivation of history and archaeology, tried to foster the sense of identity of the Turks with the country they inhabited. By our own day, Turkey has made a probably irreversible choice for a democratic patriotism of the Western European type.

In Israel and Iran also, the recovery of the ancient past has proceeded rapidly and contributed significantly to the growth of patriotism, albeit of a somewhat mythopoeic nationalist tinge. In Israel, archaeology has become a national passion, expressing the deep-rooted desire to establish continuity with the ancient past and to forget the many centuries of the Exile. In Iran, after the triumph of the Islamic revolution in 1979, there was a sharp reaction against the shah's brand of patriotism, and zealots with axes even went to the ruins of Persepolis to deface the faces of the surviving images. Yet it soon became apparent that the new regime had not entirely abandoned patriotic themes or the national interest. The Ayatollah Khomeini had proclaimed that there are no frontiers in Islam, but when the sultan of Oman requested the return of three islands in the Persian Gulf that had been seized by the shah, his request was refused. More remarkably, the constitution of the new Islamic republic lays down that the president must be of Iranian birth and origin—more than is required for the presidency of the United States, where birth is sufficient. During the long war with Iraq, it became clear that although the rhetoric was almost entirely religious, the sentiment of patriotism, of the defense of "the pure soil of Iran," was also a powerful force.

For the Arab lands, the cult of antiquity raised special problems. At first, the revival of interest in the pharaohs in Egypt was paralleled in the Fertile Crescent; the Assyrians and Babylonians in Iraq, the Phoenicians in Lebanon, the Aramaeans in Syria—all were claimed with pride by the present-day inhabitants of these countries. But soon these movements were drowned by the rising tide of Arabism. The Syrian constitution of 1950 proclaimed that Syria is "part of the Arab nation." The same formula was later adopted in Egypt, Iraq, and Kuwait. For the pan-Arabists, not only the pharaonism, as they called it, of the Egyptians, but also similar movements in other countries were parochial, separatist, and harmful to the cause of Arab unity. These movements were contemptuously designated as Shuʿūbiyya, a reconditioned medieval term meaning, roughly, national factionalism. Sometimes they were actively opposed, as in Syria under the United Arab Republic, when the Adonis cinema in Damascus was renamed the Balqīs and any reference to Aramaean civilization was regarded as evidence of support for the dissident, anti-pan-Arab, Syrian Popular party. At other times they were, so to speak, taken over, as in the attempt to prove that Hammurabi and the rest were Arabs, by granting posthumous, honorary Arab nationality to all the ancient Semitic peoples except two: Israel and Ethiopia. Nationalist historiography is generally worthless to the historian, except the historian of nationalism, for whom it can be very instructive indeed.

For a time, Arabism was the dominant ideology, even in the land of the pharaohs, where the ancient and illustrious name of Egypt itself was for a while officially abandoned. But even at the height of Nasser's pan-Arabism, the reality of Egypt survived the name. One of the most fascinating problems confronting the student of United Arab foreign policy is the relative importance of Egyptian and United Arab interests. The same policies can be and have been described as the exploitation of Arabism for Egyptian imperialist purposes, or as the subordination of Egyptian national interests to pan-Arab dreams.

In Iraq, alone among the eastern Arab states, the position is complicated by the presence of an important non-Arab minority, the Kurds. At one time it seemed that Kurds and Arabs might live together in an Iraqi nation, in the same kind of association as the Celts and Anglo-Saxons in Britain. That hope, and the tolerant atmosphere that encouraged it, dwindled with the rise of ethnic nationalism, which affected both parties.

The Arab successor states of the Ottoman Empire are now three-quarters of a century old and have become familiar and accepted. A complex body of interests has grown up around each of them; all have a strong desire for separate survival. This is especially so where the modern states coincide with ancient distinctions and rivalries— for example, between the valleys of the Nile and of the twin rivers of Mesopotamia. It is noteworthy that despite the desire for a larger unity, no independent Arab state has disappeared. The rulers of these countries frequently appear to be guided in their policies by the interests of their states and countries rather than those of the pan-Arab cause. But such allegiances and policies, however deeply felt and effectively maintained, were rarely openly avowed. They remained tacit, even surreptitious, while Arab unity long remained the sole publicly acceptable objective of statesmen and ideologues alike.

It is no longer. For some time, circumstances seemed to favor the pan-Arab cause. One of these was language. In the past, the unity of language of the Arab countries had to a large extent been theoretical rather than real. Although they shared a written language, few could write, and the spoken languages of the various Arab countries differed greatly from one another, rather as if medieval France, Italy, Spain, and Portugal had kept their various languages for conversation only and had continued to read and write Latin. In recent years, the growth of education and the consequent rise in the level of literacy have greatly increased the effect of the common written language as a medium of unity. Its effect has been further accentuated by the rapid growth of the mass media—television, radio, films, and the printed word, including books, magazines, and newspapers. Publications emanating from the two main cultural centers, Cairo and Beirut, circulated all over the Arab world, and Egyptian films brought a knowledge of Egyptian Arabic to virtually all Arab countries. The pan-Arab cause was further helped by the powerful legal and public sponsorship accorded to it by Arab governments and by the adoption of pan-Arabism as the official program of at least one major party, the Ba'th, and its encouragement by others. The public and formal acceptance of pan-Arabism has indeed gone so far that it is included in the constitutions of many Arab countries.

This inclusion of pan-Arabism in the constitutions, alongside the guarantees of personal liberty, freedom of expression, and other democratic rights, was perhaps a sign of its decline, for in the current political tradition of the region, the enactment of political principles was a substitute for their enforcement, not a means of ensuring it. In fact, with one exception, all attempts to create larger units by merging existing Arab states have so far failed. The most ambitious of these was the union of Syria and Egypt in the United Arab Republic. This was brought about in 1958 amid great rejoicing in the pan-Arab camp. It proved a difficult association and ended in 1961 with the separation of the two and the resumption of a separate existence by Syria. Other attempts to create greater units, by joining Jordan and Iraq, Egypt and Libya, Egypt and Sudan, were without result. The one exception was the union, or rather reunion, of North and South Yemen in 1990: the restoration of an old historic and political entity that had been artificially sundered by the British colonization of Aden.

While paying lip service to pan-Arab ideals, the various governments of Arab countries pursued their own separate interests, and these precluded the subordination of their own states and governments to larger centralized units located elsewhere. As pan-Arabism declined, the individual states became more solid and more real. To begin with, most of them were artificial enough, carved out of former provinces of the Ottoman or Western empires, with frontiers that were lines drawn on maps by European statesmen. Some of the entities are old and authentic. None can doubt the millennial reality of Egypt as a nation and a civilization. The centuries-old monarchies of Morocco and, until recently, of Yemen have through the centuries formed and developed their own strong regional traditions. In a different way, the mountaineers of Lebanon and the desert sheikhs of Arabia had preserved, even under Ottoman rule, strong local traditions of distinctive culture, combined with a measure of de facto political independence. In most of the countries that now form the Arab world, however, there has for centuries been no tradition of separate existence or even of regional autonomy. Their very names reveal their artificiality.

In time, all these states, however artificial in their origins, became realities. Around each of them there grew up a ganglion of interests, careers, and loyalties, and, most important of all, a ruling and administering elite that made the state an effective unit, unwilling to surrender or share power or control and increasingly conscious of a separate identity and purpose. This was already clear in the disunity of the Arab states that sent their armies into Palestine in 1948, even at the moment of crisis. It became much clearer in the years that followed, more especially after the political and social transformations that took place in some of these countries and intensified the conflicts of interest and purpose between them. The response of the Arab states to the wars of 1967, 1973, and 1982 illustrated the rapidly declining interest of the Arab states in pan-Arab concerns and specifically in the fate of the Palestinians. Between 1980 and 1988, Iraq, an Arab state, was at war with Iran, a non-Arab state. In this war, which the Iraqis presented as a struggle for Arabism, they were able to obtain financial and logistical help from some Arab states and military help from none, whereas the Iranians could count on friendly neutrality and positive support in other Arab lands. Even more dramatic were the events of the Gulf War of 1990 to 1991, when an Arab state invaded, conquered, and annexed another Arab state and thus initiated what was—despite the intervention of outside powers—essentially an inter-Arab war.

The state of the Arab world in the last decade of the twentieth century suggests an obvious parallel with Spanish America after the end of Spanish rule. There, too, the ending of empire left a series of independent states akin in language, culture, religion, and way of life. They might have come together, as did the English speaking colonies of North America, to form one or two major states. But they did not do so, and the opportunity, once lost, did not come again. The Arab states seem to be moving in the same direction as South America—a community of language, culture, religion, and, to some extent, institutions and way of life, with a common Arabism that may be equivalent to the *Hispanidad* of the Spanish-speaking world—but no more. This would not preclude the formation of regional groupings, of a pattern increasingly common in the world today, based on practical rather than on ideological considerations. It may well be that at some future time, with the growth of cultural links, communications, and the trend toward the formation of larger entities, the Arab countries may come together in larger political formations. But for the time being, the trend is in the opposite direction.

The decline of pan-Arabism was probably accelerated by the discovery of oil in some, though by no means all, Arab countries, and the consequent uneven distribution of the newly acquired wealth. In a family in which some members are immensely rich while others remain abysmally poor, the ties of kinship are likely to break if too much strain is put on them. Another reason for the decline of pan-Arabism has been the Arabs' increasing disillusionment with successive attempts to achieve it. All too often, it seemed that the real objective of the pan-Arab leaders was not so much unity as hegemony. Some chose a German model, each seeing himself as Bismarck and his country as Prussia, with a dominant role to play in the united Arab state. Others chose a revolutionary model and tried to displace their fellow Arab rulers by subversion.

In most of the Middle East, identity is experienced and recognized, loyalty is claimed and given, at three levels. The most visible, and usually the most effective, is the level of the nation-state: the central government exercising sovereign authority over the national territory and operated by a political elite enjoying a legal monopoly of coercive authority and armed force. Below the level of the state, there may be a variety of other loyalties determined by other identities. As the state disintegrates, the loyalties that it once commanded revert to older and deeper identities, more restricted and correspondingly more intense. These in turn may break up into still smaller units: from national to ethnic to tribal, from patriotic to regional to local, from religious to sectarian to factional. When, for whatever reason, the state fails or falters, these older, narrower loyalties reappear and reassert their more primal claims, often in conflict with one another. This is what happened when the government of Lebanon disintegrated into civil war, and what almost happened after the cease-fire in Iraq in February 1991. Yet despite these well-known dangers, there have always been many who yearned for something greater and nobler than the often squalid politics or shabby tyrannies of the states under which they live—some vaster, more authentic human community that would have both historic resonance and significant worldly power. The idea of Arab revival and unity, which seemed for a while to offer such a prospect, is for the moment at least dimmed. But the hope of Islamic unity remains.

5

The Revolt of Islam

On 2 November 1945, political leaders in Egypt called for demonstrations on the anniversary of the Balfour Declaration. These rapidly developed into anti-Jewish riots, in the course of which a Catholic, an Armenian, and a Greek Orthodox church were attacked and damaged. What, it may be asked, had Catholics, Armenians, and Greeks to do with the Balfour Declaration?

A few years later, on 4 and 5 January 1952, during the struggle in the canal zone in Egypt, anti-British demonstrations were held in Suez. In their course, a Coptic church was looted and set on fire, and some Copts were killed by demonstrators. The Copts, though Christians, are unquestionably Egyptian—none more than they—and it is certain that no attack on them was intended or desired by the Egyptian nationalist leaders. Yet, in the moment of crisis and passion, the mob in fury felt instinctively that their own Arabic-speaking but Christian compatriots and neighbors were on the other side, and they acted accordingly. For both these incidents there may be explanations deriving from local circumstances. But both undoubtedly reflect a common Muslim perception, that the basic division of the world is into two groups, the Muslims and the rest, and that the subdivisions of the latter are ultimately unimportant. It is in the same spirit that the Algerians found their response to the French slogan of "Algérie française," not "Algérie arabe" or "Algérie algérienne," but "Algérie musulmane," Muslim Algeria.

From the beginnings of Western penetration in the world of Islam until our own day, the most characteristic, significant, and original political and intellectual responses to that penetration have been Islamic. They have been concerned with the problems of the faith and the community overwhelmed by infidels, rather than of the nation or country overrun by foreigners. The most powerful movements of reaction and revolt, those that have aroused the strongest passions and evoked the widest response, have also been religious or communal in origin and often also in expression. In its long confrontation with the civilization of the West, the Islamic world has gone through successive phases of revival and resistance, response and rejection. Until the rise of nationalism in the nineteenth and, in some areas, in the twentieth century, it was in religious terms that problems were formulated and different solutions propounded and argued. In the period when nationalism and other Western-derived ideologies dominated political thought in Middle Eastern countries, religious sentiments and loyalties did not figure prominently in the programs and manifestos and polemics of modernizing politicians and professors, journalists, and intellectuals. They retained, however, their hold on the mass of the population, and particularly on the small merchants and craftsmen of the cities. In times of stress and disillusionment, they assumed a new importance and urgency. There was a time, not so long ago, when many were willing to assert that the secularization of political discourse in the modern Middle East had passed the point of no return. But few would be rash enough to make such an assertion today.

An Israeli scholar defined the difference between the religious and nationalist approaches to events in this way: "As believers in a religion, our forefathers gave praise to God for their successes, and laid the blame for their failures on their sins and shortcomings. As members of a nation, we thank ourselves for our successes, and lay the blame for our failures on others."[1]

The first reactions by Muslim thinkers to the facts of the decline and relative weakness of Islam were, in this sense, religious and not national. In Turkey, a series of memorialists examined the ways in which the state had fallen away from the high standards of the past and made recommendations on how to return to them. They had little or no effect. The really crucial new developments occurred among the Muslims in India who, during the seventeenth and eighteenth centuries, exercised a little-known but very important influence on their coreligionists in the Middle East.

In India, where the Portuguese had arrived at the end of the fifteenth century, followed later by the Dutch, the English, the French, and others, there was an authentic religious revival, which brought new life and vigor to the Islamic faith and community. It was associated with the Naqshbandī order, a Sufi brotherhood of Central Asian origin, which became the vanguard of renascent traditional Islam. Islam in India was gravely weakened by laxness, heresy, and eclecticism; it was threatened by both the insidious return of Hinduism and the militant Catholicism of the Portuguese. The great religious teacher Sheikh Ahmad Sirhindī (1564–1624), concerned with the syncretism of Akbar rather than with any direct infidel threat, tried to show how a measure of mystical faith could be combined with the intellectual discipline of orthodox theology and the social discipline of the holy law. An outstanding figure among his successors was Shah Walīullāh of Delhi (1703–1765), whose lifetime coincided with the collapse of Muslim power and morale in India, following the breakup of the Mogul Empire, and who, like Sirhindī, tried to bring new unity and vigor to the faith at a time of division and discouragement.

The militant revivalism of the reformed Naqshbandī order spread to the Middle East, to which it was brought from India. As early as 1603/1604, the Indian Sheikh Tāj al-Dīn Sambalī, a rival of Sirhindī and a codisciple of his Central Asian teacher, settled in Mecca, where he translated a number of Naqshbandī works from Persian into Arabic. Other disciples and preachers followed. Such, for example, was Murād al-Bukhārī (1640–1720), a native of Central Asia who went to India in his youth and was initiated there into the Naqshbandī order. He later traveled extensively in Turkey and the Arab lands, settling in Damascus in about 1670. He played a role of some importance in introducing and establishing the reformed Naqshbandī order in the Ottoman Empire. His work was continued by his son and descendants. A contemporary of some importance was the mystic theologian, teacher, and traveler ʿAbd al-Ghanī al-Nābulusī (1641–1731), a native of Nābulus in Palestine and a recruit to the Naqshbandī order. He had many pupils. Shah Walīullāh himself had in several works used Arabic instead of the more customary Persian, thus deliberately addressing himself to a larger, Middle Eastern Islamic public. One of his pupils, Sheikh Muḥammad Murtaḍā al-Zabīdī of Bilgram (1732–1791), went to Arabia and then to Egypt, where he made an important contribution to the revival of Arabic learning toward the end of the eighteenth century. Shah Walīullāh's son Shah ʿAbd al-Azīz continued his work. One of his pupils was the Kurdish Sheikh Khālid Ḍiyā al-Dīn al-Baghdādī (1775–1826), who visited India in 1809.

Shah Walīullāh himself was strongly drawn to Arabia and the Arabs. "We are strangers in this land [of India]," he wrote in his testament,

> Our fathers and grandfathers came to live here from abroad. For us
> Arab descent and the Arabic language are causes of pride, because
> these two things bring us nearer to the Lord of the First and the
> Last, the noblest of Prophets and Apostles.... We must give thanks
> to God for his supreme grace by holding on as much as possible to
> the customs and traditions of the ancient Arabs, from whom the
> Prophet came and to whom he addressed himself, and by safe-
> guarding ourselves from the penetration of Persian traditions and
> Indian habits.[2]

Arabia, for him, was the source of the authentic, original Islam, undefiled by Persian and Indian accretions. In 1730 he went to the Hijaz, where he stayed for a year, studying tradition and Mālikī law under Arab teachers; in May 1732 he went on a second pilgrimage and returned to Delhi at the end of the year.

Shah Walīullāh's idealization of the Arabs and their faith, coming at a time when the empire of their Turkish masters seemed to be in the last stages of decrepitude, must have evoked a ready response among his teachers and fellow students in Arabia. There is, however, no direct evidence of influence or contact between him and his contemporary Muḥammad ibn ʿAbd al-Wahhāb (1703–1787), the founder of the Wahhābī religious movement. Muḥammad b. ʿAbd al-Wahhāb was a Najdī who studied in Medina at about the same time as Shah Walīullāh, spent some time in Basra, and eventually returned to Najd. In 1744, with the support of the local amīr of the house of Suʿūd, he launched a campaign of militant, puritanical revivalism. His object was to restore the pure Islam of ancient Arabia by removing all subsequent accretions and distortions, notably the saint worship and other idolatrous innovations of the Sufis. The attack was extended to the ordinary Sunni schools, which in his view were contaminated by heretical practices and ideas. The Saudi amīrs of Darʿiyya enthusiastically adopted the Wahhābī cause and dedicated themselves to promoting it by force of arms. After conquering much of central and eastern Arabia, they found themselves, at the end of the eighteenth century, face to face with the Ottoman Empire. Accepting the challenge, they raided Iraq, sacked

Karbalā', and in 1804 to 1806 captured and purged the holy cities of Mecca and Medina. The Saudi amīr sent a defiant letter to the Ottoman sultan, denouncing him as a heretic and a usurper. The sultan at last took action and arranged with the pasha of Egypt to send an expeditionary force to Arabia to destroy the Wahhābī power. The task was completed in 1818, when the Saudi capital was occupied and the Saudi amīr was sent to Istanbul to be beheaded. The Wahhābī Empire was destroyed, but the Wahhābī faith lived on, to enjoy more than one revival and to exercise a considerable, if indirect, influence beyond the borders of Arabia.

The Wahhābī movement in the eighteenth century is in many ways significant. At a time when the Ottoman Empire was suffering defeat and humiliation at the hands of Christian enemies, the Wahhābī revolution marks a first withdrawal of consent from Ottoman Turkish supremacy. Although without any conscious or explicit Arabism, it was a movement of Arabs directed against the predominantly Persian and Turkish ideas and practices that had reshaped Islam since the Middle Ages, and the first considered rejection of the Ottoman Turkish right to govern. The Naqshbandī influence from India had revitalized Arab religion and the Arabic religious sciences; the Wahhābīs, perhaps stimulated by the Indian revival, went a step further and showed the way to an activist, militant attack on the religious and political order that, so they believed, had brought Islam to its present parlous condition. Although the Wahhābī state collapsed and the full Wahhābī doctrine found few converts in the Middle East, the religious revivalism that it brought influenced Muslims in many lands and helped infuse them with a new militancy in the impending struggle against European invaders.

During the second quarter of the nineteenth century, this struggle was engaged in many parts of the Muslim world. Akif Efendi, an Ottoman official, saw the danger clearly. In a memorandum of 1822 he describes the imminent threat to the Ottoman Empire and urges its people to defend themselves; otherwise they would suffer the fate of the Crimeans and Tatars conquered by Russia and of the Indians conquered by England and be reduced to servitude.

The attack, when it came, was not on the central lands in the Middle East, but on certain outlying areas; the resistance was led and inspired not by sultans or ministers, generals or ulema, but by popular religious leaders, who were able to evoke and direct strong passions and great energies.

Three of these leaders in particular are outstanding: the near contemporaries Aḥmad Brelwī of northern India, Shamil of Daghistan, and ʿAbd al-Qādir of Algeria. They have much in common. All three led armed popular resistance to infidel encroachments— Brelwī against the Sikhs and the growing power of the British in India, Shamil against the Russians in Daghistan, and ʿAbd al-Qādir against the French in North Africa. All three were religious leaders: ʿAbd al-Qādir was a chief of the Qādirī order; Shamil of the Naqshbandī order, introduced into Daghistan in the eighteenth century and revived in a militant form only a few years previously; Brelwī was a Naqshbandī initiate and a Wahhābī at the same time. All three won widespread and passionate support and waged a bitter struggle for Islam against the infidel: Brelwī from 1826 to 1831, ʿAbd al-Qādir from 1832 to 1847, and Shamil from 1830 to 1859. All three were overwhelmed by superior force, and their countries were pacified and incorporated into the conquering empires.

It was in these empires that the next phase in the Islamic response to the West can most clearly be seen, the phase of adaptation and collaboration. In India, where the Muslims were going through another period of defeat and discouragement after the failure of the Mutiny in 1858, a new leader arose in the famous Sir Sayyid Ahmad Khan (1817–1898), the founder of the "Mohammedan Anglo-Oriental College" at Aligarh and a pioneer of educational reform and of Islamic modernism. A great admirer of English civilization and a proud and loyal citizen of the British Empire, Sir Sayyid urged his people to learn English and thus open the way to the modern science and knowledge that were necessary for their recovery and progress. True Islam, he claimed, could not be in contradiction to this knowledge and these purposes. Where it seemed so, some reinterpretation of old principles and practices was necessary, much of it of the kind that Richard Koebner called "creative misinterpretation." It is not surprising that Sir Sayyid found many opponents, especially among the ulema, who saw in him a corrupter of Islam and a collaborator with the infidel enemy.

A parallel figure in the Russian Empire was his Tatar contemporary ʿAbd al-Qayyūm Nāṣirī (1825–1902), who tried to bring to his people the benefits of the Russian language and European science and culture in their Russian form. A student in a Madrasa in Kazan, he defied the ban of the ulema on learning Russian and set to work secretly to master the language of the empire of which he was a subject. He taught for several years in Russian schools and colleges and wrote or translated into Tatar a great number of books on science, geography, and other subjects. He also produced a Russian grammar, reader, and dictionary in Tatar, to help his people learn

Russian, their key to modern knowledge. Not surprisingly, he was made much of by Russian orientalists and others and is still praised by the *Great Soviet Encyclopaedia,* which defends him against the slanderous attacks of "bourgeois nationalists." Among his Tatar contemporaries, he was known as Uris Qayyūm: Russian Qayyūm.

It was not long before a violent reaction against this form of collaboration with the West began to develop. It was further stimulated by new moves in the expansion and consolidation of Western power. In 1858 the Indian Mutiny was crushed, and the last shreds of the Mogul Empire were swept away. In 1868 the Russians occupied Samarkand and reduced the amīr of Bukhara to the level of a native prince. In 1877 the Turks suffered a humiliating defeat at Russian hands, and in the same year Queen Victoria became Empress of India; in 1881 the French occupied Tunisia; in 1882 the British occupied Egypt; in 1884 the Russians conquered Marv and appeared on the borders of Afghanistan; and in 1885 the Germans established a protectorate in East Africa.

The idea of pan-Islamism—of a common front of the Muslims against the common threat of the Christian empires—seems to have been born among the Young Ottomans, in the 1860s and 1870s, and was probably in part inspired by the examples of German and Italian nationalism and unification. Transposed into Islamic terms, this meant the solidarity and unity of all the Muslims, not of the Turks or any other ethnic or linguistic nation, a concept that would have been meaningless to most Muslims at that time. The Young Ottomans spoke frequently of the union of Islam (*ittiḥād-i Islām*) as an important common goal of Muslims and reproached the Ottoman government for failing to help the Central Asian Khans when they were being overwhelmed by Russia. Bonds with outlying provinces like Egypt and Tunisia must, they said, be tightened, and closer relations established with the rest of the Muslim world, of which the Ottomans are the natural leaders. Namık Kemal's pan-Islamism was more cultural than political and was linked with the desire for modernization. Since the Ottoman Empire was the seat of the caliphate and was the most advanced of the Muslim states and the nearest to Europe, it was the natural center of the future Islamic union. "When that happens, the light of knowledge will radiate from this centre to Asia and Africa."[3] Others, like Ali Suavi, preached a more militant brand of pan-Islamism, and in 1876 the first Ottoman constitution formally claimed the "high Islamic caliphate" as belonging to the Ottoman house.

The history of Ottoman political pan-Islamism, embodied in the notion of the caliphate, may be dated from the treaty of Küçük-Kaynarca of 1774, when for the first time the Ottoman sultan put forward a claim to religious jurisdiction over Muslims *outside* his dominions. This was partly a face-saving counterclaim to the czar's right of intervention for the Russian church in Istanbul, abusively extended to a kind of protectorate over the Ottoman Orthodox Christians. It was also partly an attempt to preserve some link with the Crimean Tatars, whose political allegiance the sultan formally renounced in the treaty. It was a few years after this that we first encounter the story that the caliphate was transferred by the last Abbasid caliph to the Ottoman sultan Selim I, after his conquest of Egypt in 1517. The purpose of this story—unknown to previous historiography, whether Turkish or Arab—was clearly to provide support for this new claim.

In the late eighteenth and early nineteenth centuries, the claim was still regarded as new and controversial. Thus, for example, an English writer in 1819, speaking of some tactless German tourists with a gift for asking awkward and dangerous questions, remarks that "they would scarce have neglected the opportunity had it offered of enquiring of the Sultan himself whether he was legitimate heir to the Caliphate, as he asserted." In another passage in the same book, an Egyptian commenting on the universal dishonesty of officials remarks that even the sultan "cheated Allah himself, when he assumed the title of Caliph of the Faithful."[4]

Nevertheless, the claim was made and repeated and gained force as the other Sunni sovereigns who might have contested it were subjected to or threatened by foreign conquest. It found symbolic expression in the ceremony of the girding of the sword on the accession of a new sultan. In the past, a variety of swords preserved among the sacred relics in the palace had been used for this ceremony. In 1808, Mahmud II, like many of his predecessors, was girded with the swords of the Prophet and Osman I, symbolizing the religious and dynastic aspects of his office. In 1839, Abdülmejid was girded with only one sword, that of the caliph Omar, and the contemporary Ottoman imperial historiographer makes the significant and demonstrably false statement that this was "ancient Ottoman practice."[5] At the accession of Abdülaziz in 1861, the sword of Omar was again used, and the point was made clear by the historian Cevdet:

This sword was the blessed sword of the caliph Omar . . . which was in the possession of that Abbasid caliph who fled to Egypt at the time when [the Mongol] Hulagu occupied Baghdad. It was used to consecrate the Abbasid caliphs in Egypt. When sultan Selim the Grim conquered Egypt and brought the Abbasid caliph to Istanbul, the Abbasid caliph girded sultan Selim with this sword, and thus transferred the Islamic caliphate to the house of Osman.[6]

The sword of Omar was again used in the girding of Abdülhamid, and the Ottoman claim to the "supreme Islamic caliphate" was formally asserted in Clause 3 of the Constitution of 1876.

Two developments, coming together, seemed to have greatly stimulated the growth of these pan-Islamic ideas and aspirations. In the 1860s and 1870s, the Russians subjugated the khanates of Central Asia—old Muslim and indeed Turkish lands, including such ancient centers of Muslim civilization as Samarkand and Bukhara. The extension of Russian domination over these lands and the inability of the Ottomans to respond to the appeals of their rulers for help caused shock and distress among the Turks and other Muslims. At the same time, the rulers of Prussia and Sardinia, by achieving the unification of Germany and of Italy, were setting their different examples of how to unite a scattered and divided people. Some drew the inference that the Ottoman state should play a similar role and take the lead in creating a greater unity. For a long time, this unity was seen in religious and not in national terms, and early exponents of the doctrine were at pains to point out the difference between the European concept of nationality and the Muslim concept of religious community.

Under Abdülhamid II (r. 1876–1909), a form of controlled and limited pan-Islamism became official Ottoman policy and a useful weapon in the armory of the Ottoman state. At home, it helped the sultan in his appeals to Muslim and especially Arab loyalty against liberals, nationalists, reformists, and other dangerous dissidents. Abroad, it enabled the sultan's emissaries to mobilize support among Muslims all over the world and provided a lever for use against the Christian empires if needful.

A more radical and more militant form of pan-Islamism found expression in the stormy career of Jamāl al-Dīn, variously known as al-Afghānī and al-Asadabādī (1838/39–1897). An Afghan and therefore a Sunnī according to his own statement, in fact a Persian and therefore a Shī'ite, he claimed to have spent his childhood and youth in Afghanistan and received a traditional education in Muslim learning; he then spent a year in India, where he was initiated into more modern studies, and went on the pilgrimage in 1857. Returning to Afghanistan, he spent some years in the service of the amīr and in 1869 found it expedient to leave for India. This was the beginning of more than thirty years of travels and sojourns in India and Egypt, Persia and Turkey; he spent several years each in France and Russia, and he visited London.

The teachings of Jamāl al-Dīn are the expression of a career rather than of an ideology and do not cohere into any consistent system of ideas. A bitter critic of Sir Sayyid Ahmad Khan and the reformers, he opposed them on emotional and political rather than on intellectual and religious grounds: They would weaken Islamic cohesion and loyalty and thus serve the infidel imperialist. Jamāl al-Dīn had his own plans for reform and renewal, in some ways strikingly similar to those of Sir Sayyid, but his purpose was to equip Islam for battle, for *jihād*, and not for equal cooperation. Despite his diatribes against the "naturist materialism" of Sir Sayyid, his own beliefs were sometimes suspect; some of his writings suggest that his insistence on strict orthodoxy was for the masses and not for the intellectual elite, to which he belonged. It has often been said that Islam is a civilization as well as a faith. For Jamāl al-Dīn it was a civilization, potentially a world power, and only incidentally a faith; its basic demand was for loyalty rather than piety. The Muslims were to be united as the Germans and Italians were united, and Jamāl al-Dīn spent his life searching for a Muslim monarch to whom he could be a Bismarck or a Cavour. The enemy from which Islam needed to be saved was Europe, and especially Great Britain, the imperial power in India and Egypt. Jamāl al-Dīn's references to French and Russian imperialism in Africa and Asia are few and perfunctory. In his search for a political pivot for pan-Islam, he attempted at different times to collaborate with the khedive, the shah, and the sultan, but ran into difficulties with all of them. He was expelled from Persia in 1891 and spent his last years in politely disguised and comfortably appointed captivity in Turkey.

The work of Sir Sayyid Ahmad Khan and other reformers had important consequences, even among many who rejected both their methods and their objectives. Among these consequences were the spread of Western knowledge, a growing awareness of the necessity for a reform in Muslim education, and a wider acceptance of the need to reconsider and restate Islamic values in terms of modern concepts and standards. These themes are present in the writings even of the militant pan-Islamist Jamāl al-Dīn, who, despite his bitter attacks on the reformers, shared their desire to modernize Islamic society and the Islamic faith and thus to make them defensible against the pressure of Western power and the criticism of Western thought.

Far more successful in the long run in these tasks than Jamāl al-Dīn was his associate, disciple, and intellectual superior, the Egyptian Muḥammad ʿAbduh (1849–1905), for a while the chief mufti of Egypt and a leading figure in the intellectual revival of Islam. At first closely associated with Jamāl al-Dīn in his political pan-Islamism, Muḥammad ʿAbduh soon began to follow a line of his own. For him, politics, even the central problem of independence from foreign domination, is of secondary importance; both patriotism and nationalism are suspect in his eyes, since they tend to weaken the religious bond of brotherhood that binds all Muslims together and forms their true identity and solidarity: "He who professes the Muslim faith, once his belief is firm, ceases to concern himself with his race or nation; he turns away from sectional ties to the general bond, the bond of the believer."[7]

The first concern of the Muslim, then, is Islam, which educates, civilizes, and identifies him, makes him what he is, and seeks to make him better. But Islam has fallen on bad days; through internal weakness and error, through external pressure and influence, Islamic values have been corrupted and distorted and must be restored and defended if they are to withstand the attack of Western criticism and survive the competition of Western ideas. It was to this task, to the construction and elaboration of a system of Islamic principles and values related to the needs and conceptions of his time, that Muḥammad ʿAbduh dedicated his life.

A book by a professor at Al-Azhar University on the relation of modern Islamic thought to Western imperialism distinguished two main trends, to which the author, drawing on the terminology of our time, gives the names of collaboration and resistance. The collaborationist trend is represented by Sir Sayyid Ahmad Khan and the Qadiani Ahmadiya sect; the resistance consists of Jamāl al-Dīn and Muḥammad ʿAbduh.[8]

Resistance to Christian and post-Christian Western intellectual and spiritual influences was no doubt one of the main purposes of Muḥammad ʿAbduh's thought and teaching. His insistence on the need to cast off the accretions of postclassical Islam and to return to the pure, unadulterated, and uncorrupted faith and practice of the early Muslims is reminiscent of the teaching of the Naqshbandī revivalists and Wahhābī puritans by whom, directly or indirectly, he was certainly influenced. The movement of ideas that he led is indeed known, from this characteristic doctrine, as the Salafiyya, those who follow the Salaf, the great ancestors. But Muḥammad ʿAbduh was neither a mere fanatic nor a mere reactionary and offered his people something more substantial than empty hatred of the infidel or the mirage of a return to a largely mythical past. While rejecting the excessive subservience to Western civilization of some modernists and reformers, he was perfectly willing to accept modern science and technology and modern methods of education and even to take account of modern thought as well as knowledge in a reformulation of Islamic doctrine.

Muḥammad ʿAbduh's struggle for Islam was essentially pacific, concerned with religious, ethical, and cultural matters, not with politics or war. Armed religious resistance to the domination of the West or of Westernized regimes, of a simpler and more militant kind, still flared up from time to time in remote or outlying areas. The action of the Sanūsi order in Libya against first the Ottomans and then the Italians, the revolt of the Mahdī in the Sudan against Turco-Egyptian rule and European encroachment, Māʾ al-ʿAynayn in Mauritania and the so-called Mad Mullah of Somaliland are all examples of such movements, reminiscent of Shamil, ʿAbd al-Qādir, and Ahmad Brelwī in the first half of the nineteenth century. It is noteworthy that all of them occurred in Africa, by now the main area of Western colonization.

In the central lands of the Middle East, religious militancy was less in evidence. It played some part, in different forms, in Abdülhamid's officially sponsored version of pan-Islamism, in the Egyptian national movement, and in the Persian constitutional revolution. It was not, however, a major factor in any of them and, in the political program of the radical elites of the time, was overshadowed by liberal and patriotic ideologies. Religious hostility to the West, and still more to Westernizing reformers, smoldered on, however, and burst into flames in the anti–Young Turk mutiny that broke out in Istanbul on 12 April 1909. Some days previously, on 5 April, a meeting was held in the Santa Sophia mosque, at which a body named the Muhammadan Union was formed. A journal, *Volkan*, was launched to propagate its ideas. These, described as a "revolutionary Islamic internationalism," consisted of a combination of extreme Muslim traditionalism, militant pan-Islamism, and hostility to the Young Turks and all they represented. The leader of the group and the editor of its journal was a Bektashi dervish from Cyprus called Vahdeti. The men of the Muhammadan Union did not confine themselves to meetings and journalism but played some part in the counterrevolutionary mutiny of the First Army Corps. The program of the mutineers and their supporters was simple: "The *shari'a* [holy law] is in danger; we want the *shari'a!*" They did not, they said, want college-trained officers (*mektepli zabit*).

The mutiny was suppressed, and its leaders were put to death. The question of religion, however, remained in the forefront of Turkish concerns and played an important part in both the intellectual controversies and the political conflicts of the Young Turk period. The journals and magazines of that time, which combined a large measure of freedom with a high level of scholarship, contain what are probably the best-informed and best-argued discussions that have yet occurred between conservatives and modernists and between the different groups within each camp. The militant reaction, for the most part, remained under cover, occasionally breaking out, as in the unsuccessful conspiracy of 1910, led by the gendarmerie officer Ali Kemal, for the overthrow of the godless Young Turks and the restoration of the *shari'a*.

The First World War, with its secondary conflict between the German-made Ottoman *jihād* and the British-made Arab revolt, brought some confusion in the sentiments and loyalties of Muslims, who were in any case overawed by the immense military power of the two groups of European belligerents. A change began to occur toward the end of the war, and it developed rapidly in the immediate postwar period. It was to some extent prepared by the revolutions in Russia, which seemed to portend the collapse of capitalist European civilization. It was much helped by the disillusionment of the leaders of the Arab Revolt, even to the point of secret approaches to their Ottoman masters, now enemies—yet co-religionists. The German general Liman von Sanders mentions in his memoirs that in late August 1918 the sherif Fayşal sent a secret message to Jemal Pasha warning him of the impending British offensive and offering to go over to the Turks in return for certain guarantees for the formation of an Arab state.[9] It is ironic that this proposal was rejected in the quite mistaken belief that it was a British-inspired ruse.

In the days of despair and anger that followed the Ottoman surrender, Islamic loyalties were very strong, and it was to these loyalties that the first calls to resistance were addressed. In their attempt to win support in Muslim lands, even the Communists found it expedient to appeal to Islamic rather than to class or national solidarity, and they cooperated, uneasily and uncertainly, with the exponents of pan-Islam, whom they tried to use for their own purposes. Despite their secularism and nationalism, the Young Turks had not disdained to play the pan-Islamic card when it suited them, and Enver Pasha had in 1918 launched the grandiosely named Army of Islam for the liberation of the Muslims of the Russian Empire. After the defeat of the Central Powers, some Young Turk leaders settled in Moscow, now the main center of opposition to Western imperialism, and they busied themselves with plans for a Muslim international revolutionary movement. In 1921 a Congress of the Union of Islamic Revolutionary Societies, presided over by Enver Pasha, was held in Berlin and Rome. Its Communist inspiration was clear.

The alliance between Communism and pan-Islamism, always uneasy, was of brief duration. Enver Pasha, sent to Central Asia to further the cause of the Soviets, joined their nationalist opponents and was killed in 1922 fighting the Red Army. Sultan Galiev, the Tatar schoolmaster who worked with Stalin at the Commissariat of Nationalities in 1918 and conceived the idea of a revolutionary international of colonial peoples independent of the Comintern, was arrested in 1923 for "nationalist deviations" and disappeared in a later purge.

The most important and only successful movement of resistance to the conquering and victorious West was in Anatolia, where a group of rebels, led by Mustafa Kemal, defied the Allies, the Greeks, and the subservient Ottoman government. The later secularism and patriotism of the Kemalists have obscured the strongly Islamic character of the movement in its earlier stages, when its declared purposes were to free "Islamic lands" and "Islamic populations"—to liberate the sultan-caliph and eject the infidel invader. Muslim religious leaders, from both the ulema and the dervish brotherhoods, were prominent among the founders and early supporters of the movement.

There were three of them among the nine sponsors of the famous Society for the Defense of the Rights of Eastern Anatolia, founded in Erzurum in the summer of 1919; one of them was a sheikh of the Naqshbandī order. When the first Grand National Assembly met in Ankara in 1920, 73 of its 361 members were professional men of religion, including 14 muftis and 8 leaders of dervish orders. In February 1921, the sheikh of the Sanūsī order in Libya, who had joined the Kemalists three months previously, presided over a pan-Islamic congress in Sivas, at which many Arab delegates were present. In March 1921, the Grand National Assembly adopted as a national anthem the first two stanzas of a deeply religious poem by Mehmet

Akif, the antinationalist "poet of Islam," who had gone to Anatolia to join the resistance. In April 1921, in occupied Istanbul, a religious service was held in honor of the martyrs who had fallen in the holy war in Anatolia, and a young, Westernized Turkish intellectual, under the strain of great emotion, was moved to reflect that the true home of his people was not "the national club, the cultural lecture, the political meeting," but the mosque and congregation, "the house, home, and fatherland" of this nation. This is strikingly reminiscent of the remark of the grand vizier and Islamic revivalist Mehmed Said Halim Pasha a few years previously, in 1917, that "the fatherland of a Muslim is wherever the *sharīʿa* prevails."[10]

The mood changed, however. The sultan-caliph in Istanbul refused to be liberated, and he and his ulema hurled anathema at the rebels in Anatolia. Islam, for the moment, became identified with social reaction and political acquiescence. The Kemalists turned from religious to nationalist appeals and went far on the road to secularization.

Their secularism was, so to speak, sanctified by success. Alone among the defeated powers of the First World War, the Turks had succeeded in defying the victors and obtaining a negotiated peace on their own terms. Alone among the crushed peoples of Asia, the Turks had been able to drive out the invader and restore full national sovereignty. The impact of their successes was comparable with that of the Japanese victory over Russia a generation earlier. The Japanese had taught the lessons of modernism and liberalism; the Kemalist Turks demonstrated the merits of secular nationalism, and a new generation of leaders in the Arab lands and elsewhere was encouraged to defy the West and follow their example. None were able to repeat their success.

During the 1920s and 1930s, the prevailing forms of expression of political loyalties, opinions, aspirations, and interests were Western—mostly secular political parties that issued programs and procured votes. The most important religious movement was still the Salafiyya, the leadership of which had passed from Muḥammad ʿAbduh to his disciple Rashid Riḍā (1865–1935), a Syrian settled in Egypt. His very considerable theological achievements and intellectual influence were for long without direct political consequences. At the same time, the attempt in 1925 of Sheikh ʿAlī ʿAbd al-Rāziq, probably under the influence of Turkish secularism, to separate religion from politics failed utterly against the entrenched opposition of Al-Azhar.

The beginnings of a more active and general concern with religion can already be seen in the 1930s, in the wave of popular literary works extolling Muḥammad and the early heroes of Islam. Notable among these was the biography of the Prophet by Muḥammad Ḥusayn Haykal, which was published in 1935 and at once won immense popularity. The lives of the Prophet and the caliphs were also celebrated in a widely read series of romantic works by the famous author and man of letters Ṭāhā Ḥusayn.

During this period, a number of religious leagues, clubs, and organizations were founded, with Islamic programs ranging from a vague, generalized expression of piety to a more or less direct formulation of Salafiyya doctrines. One of these, the Association of Algerian Ulema, formed in Algeria in 1931, acquired considerable influence and importance. In the Middle East, their role was, until about 1945, minor and insignificant, being confined to social and cultural activities without political content or direction.

The ending of the war and the resulting relaxation of Western pressures in 1945 were followed by a sudden and tremendous upsurge of religious movements, expressing a messianic radicalism of a kind familiar and recurrent in the Islamic world from the days of the medieval Carmathians and Assassins to those of Shamil of Daghistan and the Mahdī of the Sudan. During the war years, great armies had camped and fought in the lands of the Middle East, involving its peoples in the provision of their needs and the pursuit of their struggles, enriching some and disrupting the lives of others. While the great armies were still there, the expression of the resulting strains and stresses was necessarily muted. As the armies began to withdraw, accumulating resentments and hostilities sought and found new outlets.

Within a very short time, the secular, political nationalist and patriotic movements had outdated and discredited themselves by their very successes. In achieving their classical objectives of political sovereignty and constitutional government, they had shown how hollow and inadequate these were. By really winning the support of the nation—and not merely of a dominant but unrepresentative minority—they had revealed the gap between their own Europeanized political style and ideologies and the deeper feelings and desires of the people they claimed to represent. Before long, in one country after another, they were swept aside by new movements, of a new kind.

In the 1930s and early 1940s, fascism and Nazism had, to many, offered a seductive alternative to Western liberalism, an ideology that combined the merits of being opposed to the Western way of life, to the Western group of powers, and of being supported by an immensely strong anti-Western military bloc. In 1945, however, fascism was discredited by military defeat; the more or less fascist groups and associations of the Middle East broke up or changed their tune, and their leaders looked for other ways, or at least for other names.

Russia, still reeling from its mighty struggle with the Wehrmacht, was not yet able to provide them. For a while, the Labour government in postwar Britain seemed to provide a socialist and an anti-imperialist inspiration. When this proved disappointing, a resurgent Russia, then challenging the West in the Cold War, appeared to offer both an alternative way of life and a champion against Western domination. As hostility to Western power and Western ways became ever stronger among Middle Eastern populations, Marxist Communists and Islamic fundamentalists competed with radical nationalists in the attempt to mobilize and direct the anger and frustration of the Muslim masses.

For the past 150 years, Europe had provided both the objects of resentment and the ideological means of expressing it. Even now, there were some who began to look to the Western doctrine of socialism as the ideological inspiration of the next phase of anti-Western struggle. But far more significant, in the late 1940s and early 1950s, were the religious leagues, whose passionate reassertion of Islamic beliefs, values, and standards responded far more closely to the feelings of the suppressed lower classes, in revolt against their own Westernized masters and exploiters as much as against the West itself.

The most active and most successful of these leagues was the Muslim Brotherhood—al-Ikhwān al-Muslimūn—a widespread, semisecret association with a cellular organization, paramilitary youth groups, and an extensive network of educational and even economic activities and enterprises. Founded in the 1920s by an Egyptian secondary-school teacher called Sheikh Ḥasan al-Bannā' (1906–1949), who was known as the Supreme Guide (al-Murshid al-'Amm), the movement grew rapidly during the 1930s and turned to direct political action in the 1940s.

The Muslim Brotherhood was soon able to play an important and stormy role in Egyptian politics, especially in the crucial period between the end of the war and the consolidation of the military regime. For a while, it operated almost as a new political party, enjoying the support of King Fārūq against the Wafd. In 1948 its volunteer groups fought in the Palestine War; on their return to

Egypt they are said to have plotted a march on Cairo and a coup d'etat in order to overthrow both the government and the monarchy and replace them by a theocratic republic. The prime minister, Nuqrāshī Pasha, struck first. In a series of moves beginning on 8 December 1948, he disbanded the Brotherhood, dissolved its branches, impounded its assets, and arrested many of its members. Three weeks later, on 28 December, he fell to the bullet of an assassin who was certainly a member of the Brotherhood, though perhaps not acting under orders. On 12 February 1949, Sheikh Ḥasan al-Bannā' himself was murdered, in circumstances that have never been fully explained.

A period of intense underground activity followed, during which the new Supreme Guide, Ḥasan al-Ḥuḍaybī, took office. In 1951 the Brotherhood was allowed to recover some of its possessions and resume overt activities. It played a role of some importance in the struggle against the British in the canal zone and in the cataclysmic events that led to the revolution of 1952. After a period of uneasy collaboration between the Brotherhood and the military regime, relations deteriorated rapidly. An unsuccessful attempt on the life of Colonel Nasser on 26 October 1954 was followed by the outlawing of the organization and the trial and conviction of its leaders, seven of whom were sentenced to death. The sentence on the Supreme Guide was commuted on the grounds of age; the other six sentences were promptly carried out. In a statement issued on 17 November 1954, the University of Al-Azhar accused the Brotherhood of having "crossed the limits fixed by God in revelation between good and evil."[11]

The public image of the Brotherhood—partly, though not wholly, of its own making—is one of explosive violence and blind, embittered fanaticism. There is also a positive side, deriving its inspiration from the teachings of the Salafiyya, which was described by W. Cantwell Smith in these terms:

> To regard the Ikhwan as purely reactionary would, in our judgment, be false. For there is at work in it also a praiseworthy constructive endeavour to build a modern society on a basis of justice and humanity, as an extrapolation from the best values that have been enshrined in the tradition of the past. It represents in part a determination to sweep aside the degeneration into which Arab society has fallen, the essentially unprincipled social opportunism interlaced with individual corruption; to get back to a basis for society of accepted moral standards and integrated vision, and to go forward to a programme of active implementation of popular goals by an

effectively organized corps of disciplined and devoted idealists. It represents in part a determination to sweep aside the inactive reverence for an irrelevant, static, purely transcendental ideal; and to transform Islam from the sentimental enthusiasm of purely inert admirers or the antiquated preserve of professional traditionalists tied in thought and practice to a bygone age, into an operative force actively at work on modern problems.[12]

Unfortunately, these aspirations, like so many others, have been frustrated by an inability to confront the realities of the modern world, to examine its problems on the level of modern thought, and to devise solutions within the range of possible accomplishment. As all too often, ignorance and anger have found an outlet in pointless and destructive violence—the expression of a state of mind rather than of a purpose.

The same combination of idealism and violence, of piety and terror, could be seen in the Iranian organization known as the Fidā'īyān-i Islām (Devotees of Islam), which, significantly, borrowed a term used by the medieval emissaries of the Old Man of the Mountain. Although Shī'ites, they held pan-Islamic opinions similar to those of the Egyptian Brotherhood, with which they had contacts. On 7 March 1951, one of their members shot and killed the Iranian prime minister, General Razmārā. It was a visit of the Fidā'ī leader Nawāb Ṣafavī to Egypt in January 1954 that touched off the first serious and open clash between the Brotherhood and the Egyptian regime. Subsequently in eclipse, the Fidā'īs remained an uncertain and disturbing factor in Iranian politics.

Even in Turkey—in the Westernized, secularized, and sophisticated society of the Kemalist republic—militant religious opposition to the Kemalist revolution has not been lacking. Its leadership has usually come from the dervish brotherhoods rather than from the official ulema. During Kemal's lifetime, the spearhead of the religious reaction was the Naqshbandī order, members of which led several armed revolts, notably those in the southeastern provinces in 1925 and in Menemen in 1930. Later, the Tijani and Nurju movements preached and campaigned against the Kemalist revolution, though stopping short of armed revolt.

During the 1960s and 1970s, these militant religious organizations appeared to have lost ground, and in many countries they were outlawed or restricted. But they continued to work in secret, and they responded to the mood and desires of a great many people among the submerged classes in Islamic society. Even the governments, however modern and secular, often found it useful or expedient to take account of Islamic sentiments and loyalties. The pandering to the Turkish reaction by the prime minister Adnan Menderes, and the use of the Islamic Congress by the government of the United Arab Republic are two different examples. The Lebanese troubles of 1961 began to bear a disquieting resemblance to the communal conflicts of other times and places, sufficient to alarm many Christians and to join Orthodox and Maronite in an uneasy and unaccustomed alliance. Non-Muslims generally have found it wiser to accept a much reduced role in political and economic life. Some have expressed alarm, though rarely in public, at the rising note of fanaticism that is now so often heard.

The most widespread, and for a while the most successful, instrument of Islamic militancy, the Muslim Brotherhood, has been suppressed in some countries and its activities severely curtailed in others. But it was not only official repression that reduced the influence of the Muslim Brotherhood: Far more important was the rise of new movements—more militant, more radical, and more extreme. In a time of increasing economic distress, social dislocation, and political humiliation, the new radicalism held greater appeal and appeared to offer greater promise than did the more conservative teachings and relatively cautious tactics of the Brotherhood.

It has become customary, first in the Western world and later even in the Muslim countries themselves, to denote these movements by the word "fundamentalist" a term derived from the history of American Protestantism. The term is ill chosen, and the analogy that it suggests is misleading, since the doctrines and purposes of these movements and, more particularly, the issues on which they part company from mainstream Islam are very different from those that divide American Christian fundamentalists from the mainstream churches.

The protest of the so-called Muslim fundamentalists is not against liberal theology or scriptural criticism, neither of which has been an issue of any significance in the Muslim world. Their protest is at once more comprehensive and, one might say, more fundamental. It is directed against the entire process of change that has transformed a large part of the Muslim world during the last century or more, creating new structures and proclaiming new values. The reformers and their sympathizers have seen these changes as a process of modernization, necessary for survival in a world dominated by richer and stronger powers. For the fundamentalists, these changes are evil and destructive: Their values undermine Muslim morality, and their structures subvert Muslim law. Those who promote and enforce such changes are infidels or the tools of infidels. If they are Muslims by name and origin, then they are something far worse; they are apostates. The way to save Islam from the infidel is by holy war, and the penalty for apostasy is death.

It was teachings like these that inspired a number of parallel and perhaps interconnected Islamic revolutionary movements in Middle Eastern countries and elsewhere. Their two greatest successes so far were the murder of the Egyptian president, Anwar el-Sadat, and the overthrow of the shah in Iran. Both were seen as acts of *jihād* against the most dangerous enemy—the enemy at home, who seeks to destroy Islam from within. In the eyes of the radicals, the crime of Sadat, the shah, and others like them was the abrogation of the holy law of Islam, and the paganization of Islamic society by the introduction and imposition of laws and usages imported from the outside world. This, in their view, is the ultimate crime against God and Islam, for which the penalty is death. Rulers and regimes that have abandoned the *sharī'a*, though remaining nominally Muslim, have forfeited their legitimacy. They have become the enemies of God and therefore of all true Muslims. The duty of *jihād*, incumbent on all Muslims, has as its first task, before tackling any external enemies, to destroy the tyrant at home and thus make possible the restoration of a truly Islamic society governed by Islamic law. After that, with God's help, the removal of the external enemy, whose penetration had been made possible by Muslim sinfulness and weakness, would be a relatively simple matter.

For Sadat's murderers—and in general for the extremist circles to which they belong—Sadat's crime, for which he was sentenced by them to death, was the betrayal of Islam and the reversion to paganism. His alliance with America and his peace with Israel were, in their eyes, only particular manifestations of this larger and deeper evil. The case against the shah was much the same. The Egyptian radicals succeeded in destroying only their ruler; the regime survived and maintained its policies. The Iranian radicals were more successful: They destroyed the regime and launched their country on a far-reaching revolution, the resonance of which was heard all over the world of Islam.

The revolution had deep roots in Iran. The public career of its most famous leader seems to date back to October 1962, when the shah's government, as a step toward the extension of representative institutions, promulgated a law providing for the election of representative local councils throughout the country. The Islamic religious leaders opposed the law, to which they raised three main objections. First, it extended the franchise, and even eligibility, to women, for the first time in Iran; second, it did the same for non-Muslims; and third, to show that this was no mere formality, it provided a formula of oath by which elected councilors would swear not on the Qur'ān, but on "the holy book," a form of words clearly intended to accommodate elected councilors of other faiths.

The religious leaders were able to mobilize powerful support against the proposed law, which was opposed by preachers and teachers in mosques and seminaries, in petitions bearing thousands of signatures, and in meetings of both protest and prayer. The prime minister at the time sought to placate the opposition, first by trying the explain away the clauses they disliked and offering to postpone the elections and, after that, by sending telegrams and letters to the religious leaders, informing them that the law had been suspended. Some of the religious leaders were content with this. Others, led by the Ayatollah Khomeini, insisted that a private communication of the cabinet decision was insufficient, and that a public announcement was required. This was made on 1 December 1962.

Khomeini's success in this skirmish portended his later triumph; his arguments on this occasion foreshadowed his later manifestos. Granting the vote to women, he claimed, was a violation of Islamic principles and "an attempt to corrupt our chaste women." The proposal to allow non-Muslims to vote or to be elected was part of a larger and deeper plot aimed at Islam and therefore ultimately at the independence of the country. The law, he said, "was perhaps drawn up by the spies of the Jews and the Zionists ... the Qur'ān and Islam are in danger. The independence of the state and the economy are threatened by a takeover."

The incident was revealing in several respects. It revealed the nature of Khomeini's concerns and perceptions; it demonstrated his skill as both a charismatic leader and a political tactician; and it illustrated the willingness of important parts of the Iranian population to respond to religious leadership in opposing the shah's government. The significance of these events was well understood by Khomeini; it was underestimated by both the shah's government and the liberal opposition; and it was entirely ignored in the West.

Encouraged by this victory, Khomeini launched a new attack in the following year when the shah's government promulgated a land-reform law. Khomeini was not impressed by this reform, which he denounced as a fraud. In general, he had little use for the shah's forced modernization, in which he saw the hidden hand of foreign enemies: "In the interests of the Jews, America, and Israel, we must be jailed and killed, we must be sacrificed to the evil intentions of foreigners." This marked the beginning of a series of speeches, sermons, and declarations in which he attacked the shah in language of increasing violence.

In June 1963, Khomeini was arrested and detained at a military barracks. News of his arrest led to demonstrations and riots, which were suppressed only with considerable bloodshed. At first, the shah seems to have hoped that he could deal with Khomeini by appeasement. Royal emissaries called on him in his place of detention and tried to persuade him not to interfere in politics. Khomeini later related that one of his visitors, no less a person than the chief of the Savak, the shah's secret police, told him: "Politics is lies, deception, shame, and meanness. Leave politics to us." To which, according to his own statement, Khomeini replied: "All of Islam is politics."

Ten months after his arrest, Khomeini was released and allowed to return to his home in Qom. The authorities claimed that he had agreed to keep out of politics; he himself denied that he had ever given any such undertaking. In either case, he did not observe it. Ten days after his return to Qom, Khomeini gave a major address, followed by several others. Although somewhat more conciliatory in tone than his earlier pronouncements, the note of opposition was unmistakable, and his denunciation of the shah and of his presumed foreign masters became ever more vehement. When the Iranian parliament in October 1964 passed a law granting extraterritorial status to Americans in Iran, Khomeini denounced this as "a document for the enslavement of Iran." By this vote, he said, parliament had "acknowledged that Iran is a colony; it has given America a document attesting that the nation of Muslims is barbarous."[13]

Through this complaint, Khomeini added an important new element to his supporters. In condemning the extension of political rights to women and non-Muslims, he expressed the sentiments of great numbers among the conservative merchant and artisan classes and the devout poor. In denouncing the granting of extraterritorial privileges to Americans, he was expressing feelings and opinions shared by liberals and nationalists and more generally prevalent among the educated and modernizing classes. In November 1964, Khomeini was arrested again, and this time sent into exile—at first in Iraq and later in Paris—from which he did not return for fourteen years.

Khomeini's first step toward home was his removal from Iraq to Paris. Although the distance was far greater, the means of com-

munication were incomparably better. When King Ibn Saud in 1927
first introduced the telephone to his Arabian kingdom, there was a
great theological debate before the ulema were persuaded of the
lawfulness of this infidel invention. Khomeini and his followers
suffered from no such compunction. From the first, they were ready
to make the fullest use of modern technology, its military weapons,
and, in the early stages more importantly, its media of communication. The Islamic revolution in Iran was probably the first revolution in modern history that was inaugurated by telephone,
television, and tape recorder.

In Najaf, in Iraq, where Khomeini had lived for many years,
communications were technologically backward and politically cen-
sored. In France, he enjoyed the full advantages of direct dialing and
free speech. By telephone he could contact and instruct his many
followers and disciples in Iran. Through tape recordings, he could
bring his ideas, resonantly spoken in his own familiar voice, to far
greater numbers than could ever crowd into a mosque. Thanks to
television and to the willing compliance of those who operated it,
he was able to win at least the acquiescence and often the lively
support of important sections of Western public opinion and even
of Western governments.

His return in triumph to Iran early in 1979 was the culmination
of a long process extending over many years, during which the position of the shah and his regime was thoroughly undermined, both
at home and internationally, while the revolutionary forces mobilized the hopes and aspirations of millions of Iranians and enjoyed
the sympathetic support of a very large part of the international
community.

After Khomeini's return and the establishment of the republic,
Iran went through the classical stages of a major revolution: upheaval and repression, terror and revolutionary "justice," intervention and war, ideological debate and political conflict, and major
social transformation. The price of revolution is familiar, and it was
paid by the Iranians at a high rate. The returns are still unknown,
and it will be a long time before they can be evaluated. This much,
however, can be said. Among the many seizures of power that have
been proclaimed as revolutions in the Middle East in the twentieth
century, Iran has set a new pattern, by carrying through a revolution
with a long ideological preparation, careful and elaborate planning,
extensive popular participation, and a far-reaching impact in all the
countries with which as Muslims they shared a universe of discourse. Compared with these events, earlier movements that

claimed the name of revolutionary in neighboring countries pale into insignificance. Like the French and Russians in their time, the Iranian revolutionaries have played to international as well as domestic audiences, and their revolution for a while exercised a powerful fascination over other Muslim peoples outside Iran. While the appeal was naturally strongest among Shī'a populations, it was and remains very strong in many parts of the Muslim world where Shī'ism is insignificant or unknown. Like the Western radicals, who in their day responded with almost messianic enthusiasm to the events in Paris and Petrograd, events "that shook the world," so did millions of young and not-so-young men and women all over the world of Islam respond to events in Tehran—with the same upsurge of emotion, the same uplifting of hearts, the same boundless hopes, the same willingness to excuse and condone all kinds of horrors, and the same question· Where next?

The long and ultimately unsuccessful struggle with Iraq, the growing economic hardships at home, the inability of the revolutionary leadership to improve or even to maintain the standard of living, coupled with the sometimes harsh repression by which the regime maintained itself and enforced its rules, considerably diminished its appeal in the Muslim world, and no doubt also—though for obvious reasons, this is less evident—reduced its support at home. Nevertheless, despite all these setbacks, the radical Islamic movements are still able to express the fears and hopes, the discontents and aspirations, of the Muslim masses and, in times of crisis, to mobilize them for action.

This much is obvious. Of all the great movements that have shaken the Middle East during the last century and a half, the Islamic movements alone are authentically Middle Eastern in inspiration. Liberalism and fascism, patriotism and nationalism, Communism and socialism, all were European in origin, however much adapted and transformed by Middle Eastern disciples. The religious ideologies alone sprang from the native soil and expressed the passions of the submerged masses of the population.

Time and again, the fundamentalists have shown, against all their competitors, that theirs are the most effective slogans and symbols, theirs the most intelligible and appealing discourse, both to criticize the failings of an old and discredited regime and to formulate aspirations for a new and better order to replace it. Their old rivals, Marxist Communism and Arab socialism, have been discredited by their failures, the one in Russia and its satellites, the other in the Arab lands that tried it. Their new competitors, the exponents of human rights protected in a civil society and of economic progress ensured in a free economy, have yet to make their way. In their contest with the liberals, the fundamentalists have an immense advantage. The liberals, once in power, are obliged by their own philosophy to allow the fundamentalists to try to replace them, as often as they may choose. The fundamentalists, once in power, would admit no such obligation toward the liberals and would indeed see it as a dereliction of duty to allow free play to the enemies of God. Meanwhile, the religious movements can still release and direct immensely powerful pent-up emotions and give expression to deeply held aspirations. Aspirations are not programs, and the fundamentalists in office have so far shown themselves no better equipped than their predecessors either to solve the problems of their societies or to resist the temptations of power. But although all these movements have so far been defeated or deflected, they have not yet spoken their last word.

The governments of Middle Eastern and other Muslim countries have tried to give expression to Islamic loyalties and sentiments through international organizations. At an early date, they formed an Islamic bloc at the United Nations—something that no other religion has achieved or even attempted—and held periodic meetings of Muslim heads of state or other holders of office to discuss matters of common concern. After some years of discussion, the Organization of the Islamic Conference was constituted at a summit conference in Lahore in February 1974. The thirty-six founder states have since been joined by many others, bringing the total to fifty-one. The OIC has concerned itself principally with religious and cultural matters, but has had remarkably little political or even diplomatic impact. On a few relatively safe issues, the organization was able to take a united stand. On more delicate questions, such as the position of Muslims in the Soviet Union, in China, or in India, or such crises as the Soviet invasion of Afghanistan in 1979, the organization has been very cautious in its policies and even in its public comments, and its members are often in sharp disagreement. The attempt of Muslim governments, never more than half-hearted, to make Islam an organizing principle of international relations led nowhere, and the foreign policies of Muslim, as of other, states were conducted to a different rhythm.

6

~~~~~~~~~~

The Middle East in International Affairs

Foreign policy is a European concept. It arose in a world of multiple sovereign states, separate but interacting, engaged in multilateral and continuous diplomacy. Like most of the paraphernalia of modern public and political life, it was an alien innovation in the world of Islam.

For the Muslims of classical times, Islam was the one true, final, and universal religion. Ultimately all mankind would adopt it; in the meantime, they must be made to recognize the supremacy of the Muslims and the paramountcy of the Muslim state. The world was divided into two—the house of Islam (*dar al-Islam*), where the true faith prevailed and the Muslim caliph ruled, and the house of war (*dār al-ḥarb*), where unsubjugated infidels still remained. Between the two there was a perpetual and inevitable state of war, which might be interrupted by a truce but could never be ended by a peace. It would end only when the whole world was brought into the house of Islam. To achieve this, the waging of *jihād*—usually translated as "holy war"—was a religious obligation, incumbent on every individual Muslim in defense and on the community as a whole in an offensive war. In either case, it was a prime responsibility of their sovereign. In the Muslim world, there was only one state, the caliphate, and only one sovereign, the caliph, the rightful, lawful chief of the Islamic community and the head of the house of Islam.

For nearly a hundred years this worldview was sustained by reality. Islam was a single state and empire ruled by a single head; it was advancing with giant steps and seemed well on the way to bringing the whole world within its grasp. There was no reason to doubt the rapid completion of the processes of conquest and conversion by which infidels became subjects and subjects became converts. The change began with the failure of the last great Arab assault on Constantinople, in the grand style, in 718. Western tradition has glamorized the Battle of Tours and Poitiers, in which in 732 the Frankish prince Charles Martel defeated an advance party of Arab raiders from Spain, and has presented this as the decisive battle that saved the West from conquest by the arms and faith of Islam. In the Arab historical tradition—on this point far more accurate in its perception—it was the failure to capture Constantinople that marked the limit of Arab expansion and forced the gradual acceptance of the idea that there was such a limit. In time, the Arabs came to realize that they would not conquer and absorb the Byzantine as they had conquered and absorbed the Persian Empire. The capture of Constantinople was postponed to an eschatological future. The Muslim caliphs of the eighth and ninth centuries and their successors became reconciled to living with a more or less stable frontier and a continuing power on the other side of it. Before long, they also had to accept the fact of division *within* the frontier—of the emergence of hereditary, autonomous Muslim states, giving only token recognition to the caliph.

The reality had changed, but the idea remained. Islamic jurists, deeply influenced by the events and ideas of the early formative phase, remained committed to the conception of the unitary and universal sovereignty of the caliph. In consequence they were unable to equal even the tentative gropings of medieval Christendom toward an international law. There was only one caliph; the question of relations between Muslim states therefore could not in principle arise. When it did, it was either ignored by the jurists or treated casuistically under the heading of dealings between the caliph and a powerful rebel. Relations with the infidel could, in theory, consist only of *jihād*, interrupted by short truces. In fact, these "truces" were often of long duration and did not differ greatly from the "treaties of peace" that punctuated the almost continuous warfare of the states of Europe.

Just as the house of Islam was one, so there was a tendency to treat the house of war as one. According to a tradition dubiously attributed to the Prophet, *al-kufru millatun wāḥida* (unbelief is one nation). This proposition, historically speaking, is patently false, but it accurately reflects a common Muslim perception. The really important division was between believers and unbelievers; the lesser subdivisions among the latter, particularly those of them who lived beyond the Muslim frontiers, were without interest or significance for Muslims. A noteworthy illustration of this attitude may be seen in the Arabic historians of the time of the Crusades, who rarely bother to distinguish among the different crusading states and nations, but lump them all together under the generic name of Franks. The same term was still in use among the Ottomans and has survived in popular usage to our own day.

As long as the Ottomans retained overwhelming military power, they did not need to concern themselves with the trivial factions among the enemy, and the question of a foreign policy hardly arose. It was sufficient to meet and defeat them in battle, and dictate terms to them, to last until the next stage in the inevitable and necessarily victorious advance of Islam.

A change began in the sixteenth century. In 1529 the Ottoman armies withdrew after failing to take Vienna and settled down to the long and bloody stalemate in Hungary. In Istanbul, the diplomatic representatives of the European powers began their long and intricate contest for positions of commercial and political advantage; in 1535 the sultan signed a treaty of commerce and friendship with the king of France, to whom alone, among the monarchs of Christendom, he conceded the sovereign title of Pādishāh. In 1606, in the treaty of Sitvatorok, the sultan conceded this title also to the Habsburg emperor, hitherto described in Ottoman documents as the "king of Vienna." For the first time, this was not a truce dictated by the victors in their capital, but a treaty negotiated between equals on the frontier.

The seventeenth century began with a concession of equality; it ended with an admission of defeat. In the peace of Carlowitz, of 1699, the Ottoman Empire was compelled for the first time to sign a treaty on terms imposed by a victorious enemy. For the first time, too, the Ottomans tried to use the processes of diplomatic negotiation and the good offices of friendly neutrals to secure some alleviation of the penalties of defeat. The foreign policy of the late Ottoman Empire was beginning to take shape.

During the sixteenth century, a functionary appeared in the office of the grand vizier in Istanbul called the chief secretary (Reis ül-Kuttâb), usually known as the reis efendi, and concerned with foreign affairs. He was a comparatively minor functionary, and foreign affairs were only one of his concerns. During the seventeenth and eighteenth centuries, he gained in rank, and foreign affairs bulked larger among his preoccupations. He was assisted by the chief dragoman. In earlier days this was usually a renegade European Christian, but from the mid-seventeenth century the office was monopolized by the aristocratic Greek families of the Phanar quarter of Istanbul, who brought it almost to the level of a ministry of foreign affairs.

Yet in spite of these developments, the notions of foreign policy and international relations remained alien to the Ottomans, and perhaps the best proof of this is their willingness to entrust these matters to members of the Christian Greek minority. Several European states had maintained resident consuls and ambassadors in Istanbul since the sixteenth century, and their number was steadily increasing, but the Ottomans were content to send an occasional special mission to Europe and made no attempt to establish resident embassies until 1793, when Yusuf Agah set up house in London.

A few years previously, the Ottomans had made their first essays in the European power game. The empire was at war with Russia and Austria; it seemed a good idea to conclude treaties with Sweden, which was also at war with Russia, and Prussia, which could bring useful pressure to bear on Austria. Treaties with these two countries were signed in 1789 and 1790, respectively. The idea of a military alliance with Christian powers was new and, to some of the ulema, unacceptable. The military judge Shanizade Efendi denounced it as contrary to holy law, citing as authority the Qur'anic verse "O you who believe! Do not take my enemies and your enemies as friends!" (Qur'ān 60.1). He was overruled by the chief mufti, who cited the tradition that "God will help the cause of Islam with men who are not of it," as well as other legal texts and arguments.[1]

The lesson was quickly learned. Only a few years later, in 1798, the empire was invited to join the coalition against the new menace of the French Revolution. The reis efendi, Ahmed Atif, in a memorandum presented to the divan, recommended acceptance but remarked:

> Every state must have two kinds of policy. One is the permanent policy, which is taken as the foundation of all its actions and activities; the other is a temporary policy, followed for a period in accordance with the requirements of the time and circumstances. The permanent policy of the empire is to prevent any increase in the strength of Russia and Austria, which by virtue of their position are its natural enemies, and to be allied with those states that might

be able to break their power and are thus the natural friends of the empire. But in the present time and circumstances, the policy more conducive to the interests of the empire is, first, to exert its strength to extinguish this fire of sedition and evil and, then, this purpose having been accomplished, to act once more as required by its permanent policy.[2]

In the course of the nineteenth century, the main lines of the "permanent policy" of Turkey were confirmed by practice and experience. Russia, advancing relentlessly toward the south, was the main danger and enemy; any power willing and able to give aid against Russia was a potential friend. Turkey's alliances have changed, but their purpose has remained constant. After Prussia and Sweden, it was the turn of France and still more of Britain, which defended Turkey against Russia by force of arms in 1854 to 1856, by threats or diplomacy in 1878 and on other occasions. Toward the end of the nineteenth century, Britain and France were replaced as Turkey's allies by Germany, now regarded as the main bulwark against Russia. That alliance ended with the defeat of the Central Powers in 1918.

The revolutions in Russia and Anatolia, on the one hand, and the Allied occupation of Istanbul, on the other, created a new situation in which a temporary coincidence of interests brought a temporary cooperation between the two revolutionary regimes. It ended when both of them overcame their enemies and gradually returned to what Atif Efendi would have called the "permanent policies" of their two countries. Already at the Lausanne Conference in 1923, there was a chill in the relations between Russia, now firmly established in the Black Sea, and Turkey, now fully in control of Istanbul and the Straits. The Anglo-Turkish dispute over Mosul in 1924 and 1925 brought a renewal of Turco-Soviet friendship, which, however, faltered under the impact of the Communist ideological offensive against Kemal and his regime in 1928 and 1929. The capitalist depression and the Turkish adoption of *étatisme* brought some revival, which was further encouraged by a common mistrust of Italian fascist activities in Ethiopia and Spain.

That friendship came to an end in 1939, when the scanty reserve of goodwill built up during the period of revolutionary fraternity was finally dissipated by Soviet hectoring and demands. The ambiguities of Turkish policy during the war years were due largely to uncertainty as to which of the contending blocs was to be the bulwark of Turkey against Russian attack—to fulfill the role of Britain in 1854 and 1878, of Germany in 1914. It was soon apparent that

that role had fallen to the United States. The role was understood and accepted. In April 1946, in response to threatening Soviet words and actions, President Truman sent the battleship *Missouri* on a courtesy visit to Istanbul, where it was enthusiastically welcomed. On March 12, he announced a program of military and economic aid to Turkey. Known as the Truman Doctrine, it marked the beginning of massive U.S. involvement in the affairs of the Middle East and of a growing role for Turkey in the whole plan of Western defense. A new and close relationship developed between Turkey and the United States, which continued until the end of the Cold War and beyond.

At the time when the Napoleonic wars involved the Middle East for the first time in the European game of power politics and war, there was only one other independent state in the area—Iran. More remote from Europe than was the Ottoman Empire, its knowledge of European affairs was less direct, its reaction to them less sophisticated. Its problems, however, were not dissimilar. Iran, too, was threatened from the north, where the Russians had annexed several provinces and were penetrating others by both political and economic means. Like the Turks, the Iranians looked to the West for guarantees, but were usually unable to get them. Germany was too far away to offer effective help; Britain fought shy of too close an involvement in Iranian affairs. There were, moreover, many Iranians who saw in the British Empire in India as great a danger to them as in the Russian Empire to the north.

The guiding lines of Iranian foreign policy were to seek support against Russia or, failing that, to play the two neighboring empires off against each other. They acquired great skill and at times won considerable success in this latter role. But the game was dangerous, and their successes were precarious. The Iranian position in Asia was in some respects rather like that of the Poles in eastern Europe. As long as their two mighty neighbors differed, they could survive and might even profit. But if ever their two neighbors agreed, they were in danger of being submerged. This danger arose in an acute form at the time of the Anglo-Russian Entente of 1907. This agreement between their rival imperial neighbors was, with some reason, seen by Iranians as a mortal threat to their independence. The lesson was driven home during the First World War, when a nominally neutral Iran became an unofficial battleground, with the Russians from the north, the British from the south, and the Turks and their German allies from the west roving at will and skirmishing against one another. It was not until 1926 that Reza Shah, founder of the short-lived Pahlavi dynasty, was able to reunite the realm and restore full sovereignty. Again in the Second World War, the Russians and the British, in unwonted and uneasy alliance, invaded and occupied Iran, deposed the shah and installed his son, and operated the transit routes that were their main objective. To the great relief of the Iranians, the Russians and the British resumed their normal hostility when the war ended. The British withdrew at once; it took rather longer, and some American help, to persuade the Russians to go.

The independence and partition of India in 1947 created an entirely new situation. In the place of the British Empire, there were now two, later three, rival states in the Indian subcontinent, none of them strong enough to constitute an effective counterpoise to the Soviet Union. The power in the north remained, and Iranian statesmen, alarmed by the Azerbaijan crisis of 1945 to 1946 and the Soviet oil concession crisis of 1946 and 1947, began to look for a new counterpoise. The Turkish precedent showed them in what direction to look. Once before, in 1911, the Iranians had turned to an American expert for advice and help against their two neighbors. In October 1947, they turned to America again for support against the one that remained. The agreement of 6 October, providing for an American military mission and the purchase of American arms, was a first step. The Anglo-Iranian oil crisis of 1951 and the temporary ousting of the shah interrupted this process, but after his restoration, with American help, in 1953, the policy of alignment with the West was continued until the Islamic revolution of 1979, after which the new rulers of Iran adopted and maintained a position of unremitting hostility to the West in general and to the United States in particular.

At the beginning of the nineteenth century, there were only two powers in the Middle East with the need for a foreign policy—Turkey and Iran. In the course of the century, a third was added—Egypt. Under the rule of Muḥammad ʿAlī and his successors, Egypt, though not fully independent, acquired a considerable measure of autonomy, enough to permit the tentative emergence of an Egyptian foreign policy, or rather, of an Egyptian policy toward the other countries of the Middle East.

As early as the ninth century, Egypt had become an independent center of power in the Middle Eastern Islamic world, and a succession of dynasties ruling in Egypt had sketched and filled in the outlines of an Egyptian policy. The concerns that inspired it were determined by the geopolitical realities of Egypt and reveal a remarkable consistency from remote antiquity to the present day.

Under the Mamluk sultans who ruled Egypt until 1517, even nominal allegiance to an outside suzerain was ended, and Cairo became the capital of the major Muslim power in the region until the rise of the Ottomans. Rulers of Syria, as well as of Egypt, it was they who halted the Mongol westward advance and ejected the last remnants of the Crusades. Masters of Mecca and Medina, they made use, on occasion, of the title Khādim al-Ḥaramayn, the Servitor of the Two Holy Places. The claim to Islamic precedence that this implied was given formal expression through the establishment in Cairo, under their aegis, of a line of puppet caliphs claiming to be the legitimate heirs of the great caliphs of Baghdad.

All this ended with the Ottoman conquest in 1517. Egypt, along with its Syrian and Arabian dependencies, became part of the Ottoman Empire, and the title Servitor of the Two Holy Places was assumed by the sultan Selim I. But under the Ottoman sultans, as centuries earlier under the Abbasid caliphs, Egypt could not indefinitely endure the status of a province. By the eighteenth century, the rulers of Egypt, while nominally governing on behalf of the sultan, in fact exercised a large measure of independence, and despite their mostly non-Egyptian origin began to pursue traditional Egyptain policies.

A new phase began with Muḥammad ʿAlī, a military commander of Balkan origin, who made himself master of Egypt at the beginning of the nineteenth century. At home, in a prefigurement of what later came to be known as Arab socialism, he tried to establish his regime economically by abolishing the old system of land tenure and revenue collection, concentrating the ownership of most land in his own hands, organizing state monopolies of trade, and building factories and industries under state auspices. Abroad, he established relations with a number of powers and embarked on a series of military and political adventures in Arabia, the Sudan, Algeria, and, above all, Syria. Although most of these adventures failed, he succeeded in founding a new state, dynastic but also Egyptian, over which his descendants ruled until 1952.

Muḥammad ʿAlī was the first and also the last of his line to apply a really independent and comprehensive foreign policy. His successors were fully absorbed in their adventures in Africa and in their complicated relations with the Ottoman suzerain and, later, the British occupying power. Their first independent venture in the Middle East was the intervention in Palestine in 1948. The resulting failure led directly to the fall of the dynasty and the emergence of a new regime.

In addition to Egypt, there were other provinces of the Ottoman Empire whose rulers, often of local origin, were able to maintain some measure of autonomy and even to establish commercial, and sometimes also diplomatic, relations with foreign powers. Notable among these is Lebanon. The Republic of Lebanon in its present frontiers is a French creation dating from the early years of the French mandate. Feeling that the original principality of Mount Lebanon, sometimes called the Petit Liban, was too small and too weak to maintain itself, the French mandatary government enlarged its territory by adding a number of northern, eastern, southern, and coastal districts, thus creating the Grand Liban, and including a considerable Muslim population. The Grand Liban was new and, like other states fashioned out of the ruins of the Ottoman Empire, more than a little artificial. The Petit Liban, in contrast, had been the seat of autonomous Christian or Druze principalities for centuries. Already at the beginning of the seventeenth century, the Druze prince Fakhr al-Dīn Maʿn had created an independent Lebanon and had found a Western ally in the grand duke of Tuscany. After Fakhr al-Dīn's fall and execution, the Shihāb princes of Lebanon managed to retain a large measure of autonomy. The Lebanese Maronites, by now the dominant community on the mountain, formed a relationship with France and with French and Italian religious orders that continued until modern times. During the communal disturbances of the nineteenth and the political rivalries of the twentieth century, some of the Maronite hierarchy and leaders developed the habit of looking to the West, and particularly to France, for support and protection. The tradition grew up of the Catholic bastion of Mount Lebanon—the brave and loyal support of Christian and Western civilization amid the hordes of Asia and Islam. During the period of the French mandate, the French government relied heavily on this little Catholic Ulster in the Islamic East. Although many Lebanese—especially among the Sunni Muslim population of the Grand Liban—preferred the rival ideologies of Arab nationalism, many others, especially but not exclusively among the Maronites, accepted the role allotted to them and leaned heavily in their policies on the French alliance.

The withdrawal of France from the Middle East in the aftermath of the Second World War thus created something of a crisis in Lebanese politics. The pressure of pan-Arabism inside Lebanon became very powerful, more so indeed than in the neighboring states, since the Lebanese Muslims, mistrusting the motives that had led to the creation of a separate Lebanon, were not bound to their country even by the same ties of sentiment as their coreligionists in Syria, Egypt, or Iraq. Among most of the Christians, many of the Shīʿites and Druzes, and even some of the Sunni Muslims, the sense of a separate Lebanese identity was, however, strong, and those of their leaders who believed that Lebanese survival depended on the West looked for a new guarantor to replace the vanished French. To many it seemed that the United States, the greatest power of the Christian West, with its own past record of cultural and educational work in Lebanon and its own current political, military, and economic interests in the area, was best fitted to take over the French role as protector of the Christians and patron of Lebanon. It took several years before the Lebanese and others came to realize that the United States was not prepared to accept this role.

During the eighteenth century, new autonomous regimes, mostly under local dynastic rulers, developed in many parts of the Arabian peninsula. In principle, the Ottomans claimed suzerainty over the whole of it. In practice, they enforced their suzerainty and maintained garrisons only in the Ḥijāz, containing the holy cities of Mecca and Medina, and—somewhat intermittently—in the Yemen, controlling the southern exit of the Red Sea and the maritime route to Asia. Even in these, they found it simpler to leave most internal matters to local dynasts, reserving only defense and foreign relations for themselves. Elsewhere in Arabia, they were content with an often purely nominal recognition of suzerainty. The rise of the European, notably the British, maritime empires in the East, coinciding with the precipitous decline of Ottoman power, created a favorable situation for the rise of local independence.

The first, and by far the best known, of those who profited from this opportunity were the rulers of the house of Saʿūd, who twice, by conquest and diplomacy, extended their small principality in Najd to cover the greater part of central and northern Arabia. The first time, in the eighteenth and early nineteenth centuries when the Saudis' expansion was accompanied and indeed accelerated by the rise and spread of the Wahhābī doctrine, they even dared to threaten and sometimes attack the Ottoman provinces of Syria and Iraq. But at that time, the Ottoman Empire, though greatly weakened, was still able to respond to such challenges, and the first Wahhābī/Saudi kingdom was crushed. The Saudis' second attempt began in the last years of the Ottoman Empire and continued, initially with some British help, after its demise. The conquest of the Ḥijāz, including the holy cities of Mecca and Medina in 1925, gave the Saudis immense religious prestige in the world of Islam. From the 1930s, the discovery and exploitation of oil in the eastern provinces, principally by American companies, brought them vast and steadily increasing wealth. The proclamation of the kingdom and its recognition and support by the Western powers confirmed the Saudis' status in the world.

Another Arabian principality dating back at least to the eighteenth century is Kuwait, where the ruling house of Ṣabāḥ assumed power in about 1756. Strategically situated between the Ottoman, Persian, and later also the British empires, the Kuwaitis were often able to achieve a high level of prosperity and, by astutely maneuvering between their Ottoman suzerains and their British protectors, a considerable measure of independence. This was formalized in 1961. Like the Saudi kingdom, the Kuwaiti principality was enormously enriched by the discovery and exploitation of oil. Far more than the Saudi kingdom, the small principality was often threatened by larger and more powerful neighbors, to which the new wealth offered new temptations.

In addition to the Saudi and Kuwaiti rulers, other Bedouin and coastal principalities in eastern Arabia followed the path of autonomy and independence, sudden wealth, and endangerment. They include the two states of Qatar and Bahrein, the latter long claimed by Iran; the sultanate of Muscat and Oman; and the seven smaller sheikhdoms of eastern Arabia, which in 1971 combined to form the United (more accurately, federated) Arab Emirates. Some of these were involved in long-drawn-out disputes with the Saudis over an undemarcated frontier and the oil beneath it.

Another region where parts of the Arab world enjoyed some measure of autonomy or even independence was North Africa. This autonomy could, however, only in a very limited sense be described as Arab. The Ottoman conquest of Egypt in 1517 was followed by a rapid extension of Turkish domination across North Africa, reaching ultimately as far as—but not beyond—the frontier of Morocco. This Turkish expansion was in part a response to local appeals for help, in part a consequence of the great struggle between the Ottoman and Spanish rulers for the control of the Mediterranean.

Egypt was incorporated in the Ottoman system and governed by an Ottoman provincial administration from which it only gradually and subsequently emerged. Morocco remained an independent monarchy, Arabic by language and culture, entirely outside the Ottoman world. In the remaining countries, now comprising Libya, Tunisia, and Algeria, a variety of local rulers maintained autonomous regimes under Ottoman suzerainty. Unlike the princes of Arabia, however, they were Turks, not Arabs. Their armies and administrators were Turks or Turkicized North Africans, and even their language of government remained Turkish for a very long time. The extensive correspondence with North African rulers, preserved in the archives of the various European countries that had dealings with them, is for the most part in Turkish. Only in Morocco, and in the more remote mountain and desert areas where tribal independence survived, was Arabic still used as a language of government and diplomacy.

The countries of the Fertile Crescent—the old centers of Arab civilization and identity, the seat of the great Arab caliphates of Damascus and Baghdad—were fully incorporated into the Ottoman Empire. They were divided into Ottoman provinces, governed by Ottoman administrators, garrisoned by Ottoman troops, and—with some rare exceptions—controlled directly from Istanbul. Some weakening of the bonds that tied these provinces to the imperial capital during the eighteenth century was remedied in the nineteenth century when new weaponry and new means of communication gave the central government far more effective means of control over even its more distant provinces. Ottoman control of the Fertile Crescent ended only with the Ottoman Empire itself.

The Ottomans, who had ruled much of the Middle East for four centuries or more, had erected a political structure that endured and a political system that worked. They had also created a political culture, which was well understood and in which each knew his powers and possibilities, his duties, and his limits. The Ottoman system had fallen on bad times, but despite many difficulties, it was still functioning and was still accepted probably by most of the population. In its last decades, the Ottoman order had begun to show signs of recovery, even of improvement. This development was, however, deflected and terminated by the Ottoman entry into the First World War and the resulting end of the empire—the collapse of the Ottoman state and the fragmentation of its territories.

As the smoke of battle and the mists of diplomacy cleared from the Middle Eastern scene in the years following the end of the First World War, it became apparent that great changes had taken place and new forces had arisen. In the long run, they made the position of the Western powers in the area untenable. At first, however, their position seemed very strong. The Ottoman Empire had gone, and the new Turkish republic, after successfully defending the Turkish homeland, renounced all concern in the Arab lands to the south. The Austrian, German, and Russian empires, all of which in the past had been redoubtable rivals of the West, were, for the time being, out of the game. Italy was still too weak and disunited to play any major part, thus leaving a clear field to Britain and France.

In the partition of the Ottoman Empire after the First World War, the Arab provinces were divided between the British and French empires and administered through mandates, a system ostensibly devised to prepare these countries for independence under the guidance of the mandatary powers. The eastern arm of the Fertile Crescent, consisting of the Ottoman *vilayets* of Mosul, Baghdad, and Basra, was constituted a kingdom and given the name Iraq, a medieval term for the central and southern areas of the country. Its eastern frontier with Iran coincided with the former eastern frontier of the Ottoman Empire, which had finally been agreed by the Turks and the Iranians shortly before the outbreak of war. Its other frontiers were determined and, where necessary, negotiated by the British. The western arm of the Fertile Crescent was divided between two mandates: one in the north, named Syria and allocated to France, and the other in the south, named Palestine and allocated to Britain. Both names were Greco-Roman, part of the Western classical tradition. They were brought by the new rulers from Europe, where they were in common use, to the Middle East, where they were not.

Both mandatary powers found it expedient to subdivide the areas under their rule. In the north, the French, after some experiments, established the separate state of Lebanon and retained the name Syria for the remainder. In the south, the British created a separate state east of the Jordan River, which they named Trans-Jordan, and retained the name Palestine for the remaining territory west of the river. Despite some changes in nomenclature, Anglo-French domination remained secure throughout the interwar period and was maintained, with some difficulties, during the Second World War. These countries achieved nationhood and, in a sense, statehood during the period of Anglo-French domination; they won their independence when that domination was decisively ended in the aftermath of the Second World War.

Three major changes in the region helped bring about this result. One was economic, the discovery and development of oil. First in

Iran, then in Iraq, and later in Arabia, great new oil fields were discovered and developed. The Middle East soon became one of the major oil-producing regions of the world.

This in turn brought a major change in the strategic significance of the region, which was no longer, as previously, of interest mainly for the transit routes between Europe and further Asia, but became a major asset in its own right, its value increasing steadily with the rise of its oil output and the growing dependence of the advanced world, in war and in peace, on oil supplies. Its strategic importance was again vastly increased with the emergence of a new challenge to Western supremacy, first from fascist Italy and then, of far greater importance, from Nazi Germany. This challenge culminated in the events of the Second World War, of which some of the most decisive battles were fought on Middle Eastern soil. Allied and Axis propagandists competed with each other in flattering nationalist self-esteem and encouraging nationalist aspirations. Axis and Allied armies camped and fought on Middle Eastern soil, employing thousands of local artisans and laborers and bringing with them the economic stresses and dislocations that are inseparable from modern war. For the first time, local political controversy ceased to be exclusively concerned with political matters and dealt in such topics as shortages, high prices, and other indications of an economy under strain.

The war brought two important measures of regional unification, one economic and the other political. The Middle East Supply Centre, at first a British and then an Anglo-American organization, attempted with marked success to integrate the economies of the Middle Eastern countries into a planned whole. The Arab League, founded in 1944, grouped all the Arab sovereign states of the region for the purpose of common political objectives.

These economic and strategic changes greatly accelerated the major political development of the period: the rise of nationalism and the finally irresistible demand for sovereign independence. Already by 1922 and 1923, outbreaks of violence in almost all the Arab countries made it clear that a simple policy of direct rule, as applied in the colonial empires in Asia and Africa, would not work, and a new imperial policy emerged, the main tenor of which was the creation of new Arab states and the concession to them of a degree of independence, coupled with the signing of treaties safeguarding the privileged position of the imperial powers and the right to maintain armed forces on their territories.

On the whole, this policy was a failure. The concessions made to nationalist demands were always too late and too small to satisfy.

They were received as expressions of weakness rather than of goodwill, and a situation arose in which nationalist politics were conducted as a competition in extremism, making it impossible for local leaders to accept anything less than their maximum demands. When treaties were achieved, they were signed either with unrepresentative governments without the support of the politically active classes or under the pressure of an urgent external threat—as, for example, the Anglo-Egyptian Treaty of 1936, signed in the shadow of the Italian invasion of Ethiopia.

The move toward granting independence was initiated by Great Britain in the early 1930s, with the recognition of the independence of Iraq in 1932 and of Egypt in 1936. In both, Great Britain maintained a military presence and imposed a subordinate relationship, euphemistically termed an alliance. France tried to make a similar arrangement with Syria and Lebanon, but with less success, and was obliged to relinquish the mandate under British pressure in the course of the Second World War.

The sole remaining mandate, that held by Britain over Palestine, was relinquished in two stages: first the British recognition of the independence of Trans-Jordan, later renamed the Hashimite Kingdom of Jordan, and the later British abandonment of what was left of the Palestine mandate in 1948. The mandate had been received from the defunct League of Nations, and it was returned to the newly established United Nations, which, by a vote of the General Assembly, agreed to divide the remaining mandated territory into three entities: a Jewish state, an Arab state, and a *corpus separatum*, the city of Jerusalem. The partition resolution was accepted by the Jewish leadership and rejected by the Palestinian Arab leadership and the neighboring Arab states.

The final stages of Anglo-French withdrawal occurred in the 1950s. In 1955, Britain evacuated the Suez Canal zone. In the following year, the Sudan, Tunisia, and Morocco all became independent. An Egyptian decree nationalizing the canal led to an Anglo-French invasion of Egypt, preceded by a probably prearranged Israeli conquest of Sinai. This ended in some military success and total political failure. Thereafter, the retreat was rapid. Kuwait became independent in 1961; Algeria, after a long and bitter war, in 1962; the colony and protectorate of Aden, renamed South Yemen, in 1967; and, finally, the British-protected Gulf principalities, in 1971.

In retrospect, and as more evidence becomes available, it is clear that the prime motive that brought both the British and the French to the Middle East and kept them there, in the interwar period and for a little while after, was strategic: concern with the strategic and military potentialities and dangers of the region. This consideration seems to have outweighed most others. In their policies and planning, Britain and France seem to have been concerned principally with the Middle East as a buffer against enemies; as a junction, a nodal point in their own imperial communications; and as a base and a *place d'armes* in case of war. All these aspects were exemplified during the Second World War.

An obvious concern of both powers was the need to deny the area to others, which, they believed, would inevitably enter if the Western powers were not there to exclude them. A consideration of some importance for both the British and the French was the safeguarding of their other and more important imperial possessions. The British were much concerned with their position in India; the French, with their rule in North Africa. Both felt the need to protect these possessions from destabilizing forces, which they feared would come out of the Muslim Middle East unless the countries and peoples of that region were kept safely under imperial control, or at least under imperial influence.

Contrary to a once-popular philosophy, there was little concern for economic motives, nor was there any expectation of economic gain. The main preoccupation of both imperial powers seems, rather, to have been the economic costs—that is, the expense of achieving the strategic and political gains that were desired. Both powers were always anxious to keep this cost as low as possible. It was only toward the end of the period of Anglo-French domination that oil emerged as a significant economic—as distinct from strategic—factor, and even then it was by no means as important as it subsequently became.

The position of both powers had several basic weaknesses. They were unwilling to incur costs to maintain their hold and reluctant to use force to overcome opposition. In both countries, there was hesitancy, uncertainty, and weakness. Almost from the start, doubts were expressed about whether the whole enterprise was feasible or worthwhile. Even Winston Churchill is recorded as having wondered on one occasion whether it would not be better to "give the whole place back to the Turks."

The thought has occurred to others on subsequent occasions, though not to the Turks, who then, as later, would certainly have been unwilling to accept any such gift. One of the clearest and most frequently reiterated themes in the political thinking of the Turkish republic is the renunciation of any kind of territorial expansion outside what are defined as the Turkish national boundaries. There were some questions as to where precisely these boundaries were, but these were border questions involving Turkish populations—Mosul, Alexandretta, later Cyprus—and certainly did not involve any desire whatever for the reconstitution of the Ottoman Empire or the recovery of its lost territories.

As the Anglo-French position in the Middle East grew weaker, it was confronted by new hostile forces, nations and regimes still possessing that special mixture of greed, smugness, and ruthlessness that is the essential ingredient of the imperial mood and that among the British and French had given way to weariness, satiety, and self-doubt.

The decisive influence of outside powers and their rivalries neither began nor ended with the Anglo-French domination. In a sense, it lasted for almost two centuries, beginning with the invasion of Egypt by Napoleon Bonaparte toward the end of the eighteenth century and ending with the cessation of the Cold War in the Middle East in last decades of the twentieth.

The foreign policy of Israel has gone through several phases, affected more by the developing situation in the region and the world than by internal political changes. From the start, Israel clearly had far less room for maneuver than did any of its neighbors. The new state had to take account of the situation of the Jewish communities in other parts of the world, which in the late 1940s and early 1950s was still very precarious; of the implacable enmity of the Arab states and to some degree also of other Muslim states; and of the generally unfriendly attitude of the Soviet Union and of its satellites and dependencies in Europe and elsewhere. Both government and people were always aware of the terrible penalties for miscalculation, greater than for any other country in the world. The basic objective of Israeli foreign policy was survival in a hostile environment. Discussion turned only on how to achieve that end. There was general agreement that this purpose was best served by a pro-Western policy, more specifically, a pro-American policy. Indeed, the active hostility of the Soviet Union and the cold detachment of most of Western Europe left Israeli policymakers no real alternative. This policy was confirmed when from the 1960s the United States, alarmed by the growth and spread of Soviet influence in the Arab lands, began to see strategic value in the Israeli connection.

To supplement this basic policy of Western alignment, the Israelis made a determined effort to cultivate good relations with states on the far side of the Arab world—Turkey, Iran, and Ethiopia nd other African states. Their successful pursuit of this policy was the more remarkable in that all these states were linked to the Arab world by Islamic or African ties and associations. Israel's diplomatic relations with Turkey were established at a very early date. Subsequently, they were for a number of years reduced to a minimal level, but were not broken off and were later fully restored. Relations with Iran were never officially established or publicly admitted, but were at one time very close in a number of fields. They were decisively ended with the overthrow of the shah and his regime. The Islamic republic has pursued a policy of uncompromising enmity to Israel. It has, indeed, gone further than have the Arab states directly involved, since most of these have now reduced their public demands to an Israeli withdrawal from territories occupied in 1967.

In Africa, a number of states broke off or downgraded their diplomatic relations with Israel after the 1967 war. Most of these were subsequently restored. A parallel Israeli policy, of cultivating alliances, or at least contacts, with non-Arab or non-Muslim groups in Arab countries—the Kurds in northern Iraq, the blacks in southern Sudan, the Maronite Christians in Lebanon—was much less successful and appears to have been for the most part abandoned.

Thereafter, the Israeli position in international relations was transformed by two major developments, one regional and the other global. The first of these was the signature, in Washington, on 26 March 1979, of a treaty of peace between Israel and Egypt. This success was achieved by long and patient diplomacy on the part of several states. The process began with secret meetings between Egyptian and Israeli emissaries in Morocco and Romania, at which certain assurances appear to have been exchanged. It became dramatically public on 19 November 1977, when Anwar Sadat, the Egyptian president, addressed the Israeli parliament in Jerusalem. The final stages were negotiated at Camp David with considerable help from the United States. The treaty has proved remarkably strong. Despite pessimistic predictions, it survived the assassination of President Sadat, the completion of the Israeli withdrawal from Sinai, and, most notably, the Israeli invasion of Lebanon in 1982.

The second major change was the ending of the Cold War, by which the position of Israel, as of every other state in the region, was fundamentally transformed. The immediate consequences for Israel were beneficial: Israel's most implacable enemies in the region were weakened by the disappearance of their Soviet patron, while a number of more distant states in eastern Europe and in Asia, previously hostile, unfriendly, or indifferent, hastened to establish diplomatic relations.

Turkey and Iran are old sovereign states with a habit of taking responsibility for their own survival and welfare. For them, national independence has been an accepted fact, an axiom of political life, in no need of assertion or demonstration. Although their independence has on occasion been threatened, it has never been lost, and their political thinking, with rare exceptions, has consequently not been bedeviled by the problem of foreign rule and the struggle to end it. Their foreign policies, developed through practical experience over a long period, are directed toward the attainment of limited and definable national purposes and are based on a normal mixture of tradition and calculation. Both countries have grave, though different, internal problems and have endured major political changes. It is remarkable, however, that in Turkey, these changes had little discernible effect on foreign policy, which continued to be determined by the basic facts of Turkey's international position and predicament rather than by the changing moods of internal politics.

For centuries, the strategic imperative for Turkey and, indeed, more broadly, for the Turkic peoples was defense against Russia: the need to delay and, if possible, to halt the advance of Russian power southward and eastward into the Turkic lands. The long-drawn-out Turkish rearguard action achieved only limited success, and by the twentieth century, vast lands and many Turkic peoples had become part of the Russian Empire, later the Soviet Union.

In this situation, it was natural for the Turks to look westward for help. In 1914 and again in 1941, the Turks faced an agonizing dilemma when their Western potential allies were themselves allied with their Russian enemies. In the First World War, they chose the Central Powers and shared their defeat, suffering in addition the dismemberment of the Ottoman Empire. In the Second World War, this time more attracted to the West and more repelled by the Axis, the Turkish republic adopted an increasingly pro-Western neutrality, ending with a formal declaration of war on the Axis powers in 1945.

The coming of the Cold War resolved Turkey's dilemma and offered it a new international alignment that satisfied both its cultural and political aspirations and its fundamental strategic needs. From the start, Turkey was a charter member of the Western democratic alliance, with a vital role in the strategic defense of southern Europe, the Mediterranean, and the Middle East. The ending of the

Cold War seemed for a while to have ended this role, but has in its place given the Turkish republic a new importance as a bridge between the democratic West on one side and the Turkic, perhaps even the Islamic, worlds on the other.

The international position of Iran, the other old established sovereign power of the Middle East, is in some ways like—but in many ways unlike—that of Turkey. For centuries, the Ottoman and Persian empires had contended for the domination of the Middle East and had fought many wars against each other. By the nineteenth century, both Middle Eastern powers were overshadowed by the rising empires of Europe, and their old rivalries ceased to matter. The last of the long series of Turco-Persian wars ended in 1823, after which the two neighboring states managed to maintain correct, though rarely cordial, relations.

Both were in a sense victims of the same forces and confronted the same problems, but with significant differences. Iran, like Turkey, was threatened from the north and had been compelled to cede important territories and populations to the Russian Empire. But Iran, unlike Turkey, was keenly and directly aware of a parallel threat from the south, from the British Empire in India, which, while not seeking territorial acquisitions from Iran, nevertheless aimed at political and economic penetration of the country. For Iranian statesmen, the best chance of survival was to play their northern and southern enemies off against each other and to secure what advantage they could from this rivalry.

The ending of the British Empire removed one of the two absolutes that had governed Iranian foreign policy and left the country in dangerous isolation under the threat of a resurgent and now immensely powerful Soviet Union. At the beginning of the nineteenth century, the Russians had occupied and annexed the northern part of the Iranian province of Azerbaijan. At the end of the Second World War, they were in occupation of the remainder of Azerbaijan, where they set up a "people's republic," apparently with the intention of turning it into a Soviet satellite like the people's democracies of eastern Europe. By a combination of skillful Iranian diplomacy and powerful outside support, the Soviets were persuaded to withdraw their troops and to allow the reincorporation of southern—though not, of course, northern—Azerbaijan into the Iranian realm. The outside support came from the United States, which the rulers of Iran came to perceive as the successor of the departed British Empire in the balancing act of Iranian foreign policy. As Soviet power grew and became more menacing, the shah—also facing serious internal problems—relied increasingly on American support.

These internal problems illustrate one of the main differences between Turkey and Iran. The Turks had been in contact with Europe and with Europeans for centuries and had an easy familiarity with European ways without parallel in the geographically less accessible and culturally more traditional land of Iran. The Turks, in a series of changes, of which the successful revolution of Kemal Atatürk was the most important though not the first, had made a conscious choice for European culture, European society, and a European political system. The Turkish involvement first in the Council of Europe and then with the European Community represents the later phases of a continuing—even if sometimes contested—process. The Iranians, despite the growth of a Western-educated professional and administrative middle class, had made no such choice, and their modernizing reforms, though important and far-reaching, were in the main limited to the material aspects of Westernization.

While the foreign policy of the Turkish republic, sustained and consistent over a long period of time, rested on the consensus of the Turkish political class, the Western alignment of the shah was seen as a personal policy imposed on him by his Western puppet masters. Successive political changes, even upheavals, in Turkey left foreign policy much the same, but the revolution in Iran brought a total reversal.

In the early years of the Islamic republic, Islam, not Iran, was the avowed basis of identification and loyalty. The aim of foreign policy, as of all other state policies, was the renewal of Islam and the revival of Islamic power and greatness through the spread of the Islamic revolution and the restoration of the Islamic faith and law. The primary and ultimate enemy of this program was identified as America—the protector and manipulator of the shah and his cohorts and, more important, the new leader of the old enemy, the West.

The term used to denounce America—the great Satan—is revealing of how the American threat was perceived by the leaders of the Islamic revolution. In the Qur'ān, as in other writings, Satan is the great adversary, the enemy of God and of humankind. But in the last chapter of the Qur'ān, in the best-known and most frequently cited reference to Satan, the believer is urged to seek refuge in God from "the mischief of the insidious Whisperer, who whispers in people's hearts" (Qur'ān 114: 4–5). It is the Tempter, not the

Adversary, that Khomeini feared in America, the seduction and enticement of the American way of life rather than the hostility of American power. The danger of Western enticement, *gharbzadegi*, which has been variously translated as "Westosis" or "Westoxication," has long been a favorite theme of Iranian writers.

The Iranian revolution, like others before it, has gone through the successive phases set out in paradigmatic form by the French. The monarchy was violently overthrown, but in Iran the monarch escaped death, by exile. Others were less fortunate, and the mullahs imposed a reign of terror that far exceeded that of their French predecessors. The ideologues and pragmatists fought out their classical battles, and the Iraqis, with royalist support, gave them their war of intervention and their victory at Valmy. Later, thanks in large measure to Western, especially American, help, the Iraqis were able to halt the at first triumphant Iranian counterattack and to wring a kind of victory from a long-drawn-out war of exhaustion. For the time being at least, the Islamic revolution was contained, and the revolutionaries, in both their domestic and their international activities, became less like Jacobins and more like Bolsheviks. The exultant and sometimes passionate response that the revolution aroused all over the Muslim world faded and gave way either to apathy or, after an interval, to a renewed search for radical solutions.

Inside Iran, a new generation of leaders, hardened by eight years of war with neighboring Iraq, began to think more of Iran and less of Islam and to devise external as well as internal policies more concerned with the survival and strengthening of the Iranian state and with what they perceived to be the national interests of the Iranian realm. To create an Iranian national foreign policy, the rulers of Iran had to overcome many difficulties: the resistance of small but powerful and entrenched groups still wedded to the idea of universal Islamic revolution and unwilling to see it confined to one country; the well-grounded suspicion of all their neighbors and of more distant states whose goodwill they needed; and the moral and material obstacles to establishing, or even attempting to establish, friendly relations with those whom they had for so long regarded and denounced as forces of evil incarnate.

In contrast to Turkey and Iran, the Arab states were all comparatively new to independence, and their political elites for a long time were dominated by the struggle to attain it. Then there were the problems of how to exercise it, a task involving a difficult readjustment of attitudes and ideas. It was not easy to turn from the vast and ill-defined aims of nationalist opposition to the limited and practical calculations of national government. It also was difficult to accept the idea that complaints against oppression and other evils should now be addressed to compatriots and coreligionists.

The foreign policies of the Arab states have been concerned with three things: their relations with Israel, with one another, and with the outside world. On the first point, for a long time they agreed that Israel should be destroyed, though not on how this should be accomplished. In time, this position was modified, and the Arab official demand was no longer for the immediate destruction of Israel, but for its reduction to the frontiers laid down in the 1947 partition proposals—according to some, a first step toward its ultimate disappearance. Since Israel clearly would not submit voluntarily to such a truncation and since the Arab states alone were unable to enforce it, this amounted in effect to a demand for an imposed settlement by the great powers—a kind of compulsory surgery on the conference table, in which perhaps Soviet arms would wield the knife while Western diplomacy administered the anaesthetic. This was never a very likely contingency and became even less so after the 1967 war, which left Israel in possession of the whole of mandatary Palestine west of the Jordan River as well as significant areas of Egyptian and Syrian territory. The formal Arab demand was now for Israel's withdrawal from the territories acquired in 1967— that is, to the cease-fire lines agreed to in 1948 and 1949. As in the previous phase, it was by no means clear whether this was an initial or a final demand and whether compliance would be followed by Arab recognition of the state of Israel and by a normalization of relations.

For a number of years, recognition has indeed seemed very unlikely. At a summit conference that met in Khartoum on 1 September 1967, the Arab leaders announced that they had agreed there was to be "no recognition, no negotiation, no peace." This was the formal position of all Arab governments until 1978, when Egypt entered into negotiations with Israel that eventually led to a peace treaty. It remained the position of the rest of the Arab world until the beginning of the American-sponsored peace negotiations in 1991. An even more explicitly uncompromising attitude was adopted by the Palestine Liberation Organization, which, refusing to recognize the legitimacy of Israel, demanded the dismantling of the Jewish state and its replacement by an Arab Palestinian state. This was the unwavering PLO position until 1988 when its leader, Yāsir ʿArafāt, in a speech in Geneva, for the first time talked of the possibility of coexistence between Jewish and Arab states in the former mandated territory.

The emergence of the Palestinians as an independent factor and the appearance of the Palestine Liberation Organization as a major player in both regional and international affairs are among the most important consequences of the 1967 war. Between 1948 and 1967, the Arab states, and particularly the three directly involved in Palestinian affairs, saw themselves as the upholders of the Palestinian cause and discouraged any attempt by the Palestinian leadership to represent their own cause. Of the three states, the least involved was Syria, which at the time of the armistice held only the little town of al-Hamma on the eastern shore of the Sea of Galilee. The most involved was Jordan, which held the West Bank territories and the eastern part of Jerusalem. The Gaza strip, small in area but with a swollen refugee population, was held by Egypt.

The Egyptians did not annex the Gaza strip, but administered it as part of Palestine and even experimented, briefly and unsuccessfully, with an "All-Palestine Government" based in Gaza. The Jordanian government pursued an entirely different policy. Abolishing the boundary established in 1922 by British administrative action, between Cis-Jordanian and Trans-Jordanian Palestine, Jordan formally annexed the West Bank and east Jerusalem. These became part of the Jordanian kingdom, the capital of which remained in Amman. The Jordanian nationality law of 4 February 1954 conferred Jordanian citizenship on all who held Palestinian citizenship before 15 May 1948 and had resided in the Jordanian kingdom between 20 December 1949 and 16 February 1954, "except Jews." It also offered Jordanian citizenship to any Arab Palestinian refugee and his descendants, wherever born, who requested this in writing and renounced any other citizenship that they might hold. This annexation was not recognized by other Arab states, whose leaders claimed that it was tantamount to a renunciation of Palestinian rights. Apart from those in Jordan, only those Palestinians who found refuge in Western countries were able to acquire citizenship by naturalization and, later, by birth. Inevitably, conflicts of interest among the Arab states impeded their conduct of the Arab cause, and even the PLO, founded in 1964, began its career as an instrument of these rivalries.

The war of 1967 changed the situation dramatically. The Gaza strip, the West Bank and east Jerusalem, and al-Hamma all were conquered by the Israelis, who were now in possession of all the territory of mandatary Palestine west of the Jordan River. The Arab states had failed signally to promote the Palestine cause by war and other state actions. The Palestinians, no longer under the rule of Arab states in Palestine or under their aegis in international fora, embarked on an independent line of action of their own. This consisted in part of a skilled, and for a while successful, diplomatic offensive, which by the late 1980s left the PLO in diplomatic relations with more countries than was the state of Israel, and in part of a campaign of armed violence that its defenders called resistance or guerrilla warfare and its critics called terrorism.

These activities achieved considerable propaganda and political success in the 1970s and early 1980s, but accomplished little or nothing on the ground in Palestine. The use of armed violence against places, installations, and individuals with no connection with Israel, and the resulting loss of life, tarnished even the previous propaganda successes. When in 1982 the Israelis invaded Lebanon, for the declared purpose of evicting the PLO from the bases that it had established in that country, there was remarkably little opposition or protest in the international community, or even in the Arab states. The PLO was further weakened by the end of the Cold War and the breakup of the Soviet Union and by the defeat of the Iraqi dictator Saddam Hussein, for whom its leaders had incautiously declared their support. In the inter-Arab struggle that preceded, accompanied, and followed the Iraqi invasion of Kuwait, the PLO became identified with one side and therefore lost much of the support and goodwill that it had previously enjoyed with the other. It remained to be seen whether it could still play a useful role in the peace negotiations that became possible in the new configuration of forces in the Middle East and in the world.

The emergence of Israel in 1948—or rather, the failure of the Arab armies to prevent it—was a climactic event in the history of the Middle East, comparable in many ways with the landing of the Greeks in Izmir in 1919. It was bad enough to be dominated by the Franks, but they were after all the invincible masters of the world, who—on both occasions—had just defeated their enemies in a great war. It was a very different matter, and an intolerable humiliation, to submit to the Greeks or Jews, to local *dhimmīs* whom the Muslims had long been accustomed to despise as inferiors. The Franks, moreover, would, sooner or later, go back whence they came. But the Greek Great Idea—*megalē idea*—of a revived Byzantine empire and the Zionist idea of a revived Jewish state were clearly intended to be permanent. The same sense of outrage colored the Kemalist reaction against the Greeks and the Arab reaction against Israel. Some of the difference in the subsequent development of Turkey and the Arab states may be ascribed to the fact that the Turks won their war, whereas the Arabs lost theirs.

Within a few years, all the rulers who had sent their armies to defeat in Palestine had fallen, several of them by assassination. In March 1949, the Syrian chief of staff, Colonel Husnī Za'īm, over-threw the Syrian government by a coup d'état and established a military regime with himself as president. It was the first of a series of military revolutions and convulsions, which, in many countries and with increasing violence, swept away the regimes of the kings, the pashas, and the conservative landowners and unleashed new forces.

In 1945, when the war ended, Great Britain seemed firmly estab-lished as the dominant power in the Middle East, with overwhelming military force and political influence. The Arab League, so it seemed, was its instrument for the political integration of the region, and the Middle East Supply Centre was its economic counterpart. Ger-many and Italy had been eliminated by defeat; France had been in effect evicted; America was not yet willing, Russia was not yet able, to play a role. Even the nationalist leaders were for the moment silent, anxiously aware of the might of the victors and, for many, of their own suspect associations with the vanquished. It was not a moment to press demands.

Within ten years of the end of the war, the imposing structure of British power in the Middle East had been undermined, weakened, and destroyed; the British positions of strength, under attack from every side, were one by one abandoned or lost. The Middle East ceased to be an area of British predominance, and it also ceased to be an area of predominantly Western influence.

A number of causes contributed to this contraction and with-drawal of British power. One of the first was the transfer of power in India in 1947. It was as the paramount power in India that Britain first became actively involved in the affairs of the Middle East. The ending of that paramountcy greatly reduced both the need and the means for British action in the area. Another cause was the failure to solve the Palestine problem and the abdication of the Palestine mandate, a confession of weakness and irresolution that could not fail to stimulate and encourage further demands and attacks from every side. Some observers would add the inability of the makers of policy to recognize, understand, and allow for the new forces that were rising in the Arab world and elsewhere and that would sweep away the supports of British influence and power.

Underlying all these and more fundamental than any of them was the exhaustion of British power and resources after six years of war against mighty enemies. Already in March 1947, President Truman had sought and obtained authority from Congress to give Greece and Turkey the help that they needed, and that Britain could no longer supply, in defending their independence and integrity against the Communist threat from the north. This policy was soon after extended to Iran. Toward the end of 1949, the U.S. government was already considering a more active role in the Middle East as a whole. A meeting of U.S. diplomats in the area was held in Istanbul in November 1949 and was addressed by the assistant secretary of state, George G. McGhee. His remarks were summarized by one of those present, the ambassador to Israel, James G. McDonald:

> The basis of United States policy in the Middle East, McGhee told us, was to aid the development of all resources in the area, in order to lift the standard of living, and with an immediate two-fold purpose: (1) to avert the threat of Communism from the inside, and (2) to keep armed the defensible border states (Greece and Turkey) as a defence against any outside Soviet aggression.
>
> First and foremost, consequently, the United States could no longer take a back seat in the affairs of the Middle East. For, with the Communist threat mounting, Britain, hard-pressed by other problems, could no longer maintain full responsibility for the protection of Western interests and civilization in the area. The United States must shoulder an increasing part of the burden. In this respect, "complete agreement in principle" had been reached with Great Britain. Both countries, said McGhee, had the same general objectives, though in certain countries specific interests might not be identical. There were, he added, "points of asymmetry."
>
> It seemed to me that this was an understatement of the extent of the divergence between our and British national interests.[3]

During the years that followed, the divergences—not so much between real national interests as between the two manners of interpreting and defending them—became painfully obvious. In 1951 and 1952, British difficulties reached their climax: the murder of King 'Abdullah in Jordan, the oil crisis in Iran, and the Anglo-Egyptian deadlock followed by the Egyptian rejection of the four-power proposal for a Middle East defense pact and, soon after, the Anglo-Egyptian clash in the Suez Canal zone culminating in the five-hour battle at Isma'ilia on 25 January 1952.

American policy in this period and the following seems to have been based on the belief that too close an association with Great Britain, too careful a regard for British interests, would tarnish the American image and obstruct American purposes. Britain, it was argued, even after its dramatic renunciation of empire in Asia and Africa, was still suspect in Asian and African eyes not only as an ex-imperial power, but as one seeking to return. America, on the other hand, was itself an ex-colonial state—indeed, the first to win freedom by a successful revolution against British imperialism. Where America had led, others were following and would be bound to America by natural ties of sympathy and affinity.

The idea that the emergent nations of Asia and Africa would accept the American Revolution as the prototype of their own struggle against colonialism and spontaneously rally to American leadership was never a very convincing idea, and rested on an analogy that was false to the point of absurdity. The American Revolution, after all, was not a victory against colonialism, but the ultimate triumph of colonialism: when the colonists have conquered and settled the colony so thoroughly that they are able to stand alone without needing the further support of the mother country. It would be unfair and misleading to compare the American colonists of the eighteenth century with the white settler communities of today, but rather less absurd than to identify them with the white settlers' subjects.

If American involvement in the defense of the Middle East began as an effort to shore up the crumbling British defenses against a possible Soviet attack, it was in time realized that such a policy was untenable and perhaps even self-defeating—not, as some believed at the time, because the British communicated a taint of imperialism from which the Americans were otherwise free, but, more simply, because the British no longer had the strength to sustain this task.

In the 1950s, the United States took over the task, with only intermittent success. In 1952, Greece and Turkey were accepted as members of the North Atlantic Treaty Organization, thus forming a link between the system of alliances that was to defend Europe and the Mediterranean, on the one hand, and the new structure of alliances which it was hoped to construct in the Middle East, on the other.

This Middle Eastern defensive system at first consisted only of the northern tier of states abutting directly on the Soviet bloc—that is, Greece, Turkey, and Iran. In 1955, the government of Iraq was persuaded to join in a new alliance known as the Baghdad Pact, consisting of Turkey, Iraq, and Iran, the rulers of which were by now acutely conscious of the threat from the north. Britain, too, was retained as a member of the Baghdad Pact, but the United States for the time being preferred to be an informal associate rather than a formal member of this alliance, for whose creation it was in large measure responsible. Although the alliance with the states of the northern tier was successful in preventing a direct Soviet attack, it failed to prevent—indeed, some have argued that it directly caused— the Soviet masterstroke of leapfrogging the northern tier and establishing positions of strength in the heart of the Arab world.

The final stage in the British withdrawal from Egypt began in July 1954, when a few weeks after the conversations between Eisenhower and Churchill in Washington, an Anglo-Egyptian agreement was reached, providing for the evacuation by the British of the Suez Canal zone within twenty months. The last British troops were in fact withdrawn on 2 April 1955. It was obvious that the abandonment of the great Suez Canal base, for seventy years the keystone of the edifice of British power in the Middle East, would have immediate and far-reaching effects. Great expectations were placed on the agreement. At the time, the hope was widely entertained and still more widely expressed that with the removal of the last Egyptian grievance against the West, real friendship and cooperation would at last become possible.

For those who held them, these hopes were swiftly disappointed. The general situation, far from getting better, got rapidly worse. The Egypt–Israel border, after a period of comparative calm, became once again the scene of new military clashes. The anticipated improvement in Egyptian relations with the West failed to materialize. The liberation of their own soil left the Egyptians free to take up larger Arab and African causes; the attempt by the West to form a Middle Eastern alliance and persuade Egypt to join it provoked increasingly hostile reactions in Egypt, culminating in the signature in September 1955 of an agreement with Czechoslovakia for the supply of arms. At one blow, the Soviet Union had established itself in a position of power and influence in the very heart of the Middle East.

In Turkey and Iran, American aid was welcomed, and American leadership accepted. Neither of these was an ex-colonial country. For them, America was not the ancient pioneer of anticolonialism, but the new leader of the West and, as such, their natural defender against the old and familiar threat from Russia. In the Arab countries there was no such awareness, based on experience, of Russian expansionism and therefore no such desire to seek or accept Western— American or other—support. Only one Arab country—Iraq—actually entered the pact. It was taken in by an unpopular and un-representative regime, which had not long to survive. There can be little doubt that its pro-Western alignment was one of the main causes of its overthrow. In the light of what later became known of Nūrī al-Saʿīd's secret approaches to the Germans in 1940, we may wonder how effective the alliance would have been if the regime had survived and been put to the test.

Whatever its apparent military advantages, the attempt to involve Iraq in a Western defensive system can now be seen as a major political error. In other Arab lands, it aroused bitter hostility and led directly to negotiations with the Communist bloc, the way for which was prepared by President Nasser's participation in the neutralist conference at Bandoeng in April 1955—his first introduction to international, as distinct from Middle Eastern, politics. It was a portentous beginning.

The interest of the Soviet Union in the Middle East was not new. At the meeting between Hitler and Molotov in November 1940, the Soviet government, according to captured German documents, demanded German agreement to a Soviet military and naval base on the Bosphorus and the Dardanelles and recognition of "the area south of Batum and Baku in the general direction of the Persian Gulf . . . as the center of the aspirations of the Soviet Union."[4]

After the German attack on the Soviet Union, these plans were shelved. They reappeared at the end of the war when circumstances seemed favorable for their fulfillment, with northern. Iran under Soviet occupation, Turkey isolated by its protracted neutrality, and the Soviets part of the victorious alliance. On that occasion the attempt failed; the "people's republic" set up in Iranian Azerbaijan was overthrown, and the demand for bases in the Turkish straits was steadfastly refused. Apart from the abortive agreement with Mosaddegh in Iran in 1953, the Soviets made no further attempt to intervene at the government level in Middle Eastern affairs but preferred to stay on the sidelines, waiting for the "inevitable contradictions of capitalism" to disrupt the political and economic structure of the Middle East and thus prepare the way for Communism. Where convenient, the working of these contradictions was aided by what one might call routine subversion.

The return of the Soviet Union in 1955 to an active role in Middle Eastern politics was not—or should not have been—in itself surprising. The timing was masterly. The Arab states were divided and angry about the pro-Western alignment of Iraq; Egypt was bitterly hostile and had just received a flattering initiation into the society of the great Asian neutralists. Arab–Israeli relations were more than usually bad and continued to distort political thinking in the region generally. The British Middle Eastern base at Suez was being dismantled and transferred to Cyprus, which in turn was convulsed by a fierce conflict. This again had embroiled Turkey and Greece, on whose friendship and goodwill the southeastern corner of NATO so largely depended.

The Soviet move seems to have begun in April, when *Izvestya* published a Foreign Ministry statement deploring "the recent deterioration in the situation" and expressing the intention of the USSR to develop closer relations with the countries of the Middle East. During the spring and summer, there were intensive diplomatic activities, including exchanges of visits and missions with several Arab countries. Attempts to ignore and then play down reports of an arms deal between Egypt and the Soviet bloc were abandoned at the end of September when news of the agreement was officially released.

Far more strikingly—and alarming—than the arms deal itself was the wave of almost ecstatic joy with which it was received all over the Arab world. The Syrian, Lebanese, and Jordanian chambers of deputies at once voted resolutions of congratulation to President Nasser, and almost the entire Arab press greeted the news with rapturous acclamation. Even Nūrī al-Saʿīd felt constrained to send a message of congratulation and approval to the Egyptian leader.

This response was not due to any special love of the Soviets or to any desire to see either Communism or Soviet power extended in the Middle East; it was due rather to a lively appreciation of the quality of President Nasser's act as a slap in the face for the West. The president's slap and the red-faced, agitated, and ineffectual Western response to it gave a dramatic and satisfying expression to a mood and wish that united many if not most Arabs: the mood of revulsion from the West and the wish to spite and humiliate it. "Most Westerners," says W. Cantwell Smith, "have simply no inkling of how deep and fierce is the hate, especially of the West, that has gripped the modernizing Arab."[5]

The first of the postwar Arab revolutions, that of Egypt in 1952, was initially neither socialist nor pro-Soviet, but in time it became both. In 1958, a revolution in Iraq—to no small extent provoked by hostility to the inclusion of that country in a Western alliance— overthrew the monarchy and established a strongly anti-Western regime, which soon drifted into a close relationship with the Soviet

Union. The pro-Western monarchy in Jordan narrowly escaped over-throw, from which it was saved by a small but sufficient British airlift of troops.

In Lebanon, the policy of local separatism and Western alliance had always displeased the Arab nationalists, and in a time of intense national and communal fervor and of violent anti-Western feeling, it enraged them to the point of civil war. This brought the first American military intervention in the region, whose purpose—if purpose may be judged by results—was to replace a pro-American government by another that was less pro-American and therefore more viable.

The northern tier alliance was reconstituted without Iraq and renamed the Central Treaty Organization, based on Turkey and Iran. At the same time, the first steps were taken toward establishing a new American strategic relationship with the state of Israel.

In the early years of the state's existence, American policy to-ward Israel, though generally friendly and sympathetic, had been cautious and somewhat distant, principally for fear of antagonizing Arab opinion. The Soviet Union had preceded the United States by some time in according de jure recognition to Israel, and encouraged its satellites to be helpful, with decisive effect in Israel's first war, in 1948. The small quantity of arms smuggled to Israel from the United States at that time was due to private and illegal initiatives, in defiance of an otherwise strictly enforced official U.S. arms em-bargo. American financial and military aid to Israel was on a very small scale and did not reach substantial proportions until the late 1960s and early 1970s. The weaponry that enabled Israel to survive in 1948 came from Czechoslovakia; the planes and tanks that won the dazzling victory of the Six-Day War in 1967 came principally from France.

The American strategic relationship with Israel, which had be-gun in 1962, became significant only after 1967 and was a conse-quence, not—as has sometimes been argued—a cause, of Soviet penetration and growing Soviet influence in the Arab world. By the early 1970s, the Soviets felt strong enough to repeat the policies that the British had followed a generation earlier and to sign "treaties of alliance" with Arab countries, whereby they were able to establish a military and naval presence and to acquire and use military, naval, and air bases with virtually extraterritorial status. At one time or another, Egypt, the Sudan, Syria, Iraq, South Yemen, Libya, and Algeria seemed to be moving into the Soviet orbit, acquiring Soviet

weapons, accepting Soviet instructors, adopting a pro-Soviet alignment at the UN and other international fora, and—most portentous
of all—adopting a form of socialist, though not Communist, planning in their domestic economies.

There were always statesmen and even governments in the Arab
world that believed in a policy of cooperation or association with
the West. They could, however, pursue such a policy only by dis-
regarding, misleading, or suppressing popular feeling, and did so at
peril of their lives. On the other hand, the acceptance of Soviet favors
carried no such risks to personal safety or political popularity and
was far less suspect than any leaning toward the West. The same
double standard toward the Soviets and the West could be seen in
many things: in the silent, almost surreptitious pocketing of Western gifts and the loud welcoming of Soviet benefactions, and in the
ceaseless harrying of the last retreating rearguards of Western empire
while Soviet rule over vast Muslim territories in Asia passed un-
criticized. A still more striking disparity may be seen in the responses to the involvements of the United States in Vietnam and
of the Soviet Union in Afghanistan. While America's intervention
in the war between North and South Vietnam on the side of its
South Vietnamese ally was greeted with almost universal and unequivocal condemnation, the Soviet Union's invasion and conquest
of Afghanistan, a neighbor with which it was at peace, and the
ruthless repression of the Afghan patriotic resistance evoked only
the mildest expressions of disapproval in many Arab and Islamic
states and even found defenders in some of them. Despite some
subsequent improvement, the prevailing attitude toward the West
remained one of deep mistrust and hostility. Collaboration with the
West still needed to be excused or, better still, concealed. During
the Persian Gulf crisis of 1990 and 1991, it was clear that although
many Arab governments were glad to join the American-led coalition against Saddam Hussein, there was much less support for this
policy among their people, for many of whom Saddam Hussein's
angry defiance of the West more than atoned for his offenses against
his Arab subjects and neighbors in Iraq and Kuwait. The coalition
was possible only because by that date the Soviet Union was no
longer a player in the game. From time to time, the West has found—
or procured—regimes that were willing to collaborate with it, if only
in secret and within narrow limits. The difficulty was that such
collaboration was always uncertain, and the regimes that provided
it were either untrustworthy or insecure, sometimes both.

We shall be better able to understand this situation if we view the present discontents of the Middle East not as a conflict between states or nations but as an encounter between civilizations. The "Great Debate," as Gibbon called it, between Christendom and Islam has been going on, in one form or another, since the advent of Islam in the seventh century. For more than a century and a half, Islam was subject to the domination of the West, a domination that was posed to the Muslim peoples, and continues to pose even after political control has ended, tremendous problems of readjustment—political, social, economic, cultural, psychological—both in their dealings with others and in their own internal affairs. Even after liberation, the intelligent and sensitive Arab could not but be aware of the continued subordination of his culture to that of the West. His richest resource was oil, but it was found and extracted by Western processes and machines, to serve the needs of Western inventions. His greatest pride was his new army, but it used Western arms, wore Western-style uniforms, and marched to Western or Western-style tunes. His ideas and ideologies, even of anti-Western revolt, derived ultimately from Western thought. His knowledge even of his own history and culture owed much to Western scholarship. His writers, his artists, his architects, his technicians, even his tailors, testified by their work to the continued supremacy of Western civilization: the ancient rival, once the pupil, now the model, of the Muslim. Even the gadgets and garments, the tools and amenities of his everyday life were symbols of bondage to an alien and dominant culture, which he hated and admired, imitated but could not share. It was a deeply wounding, deeply humiliating experience.

In the twilight world of popular myths and images, the West was the source of all evil—and the West was a single whole, the parochial subdivision of which were hardly more important to the average Middle Easterner than were those of the Middle East for the average Westerner. Established sovereign states like Turkey and Iran and some of the older Arab states have developed consistent foreign policies based on national interests and rational calculations, but all too often the policies of Arab governments have been at the mercy of a popular mood of ethnic and communal collectivism, which treated the West as a collective enemy.

The Soviets for a while succeeded where the Americans had failed, in presenting themselves to the Arabs as something generically different from the West. They succeeded because they were something generically different, whereas America was not. America was inescapably part of the West, of which it has now become the leader. The Soviet Union was not part of the West but, on the contrary, was opposed to the West—in ideology, economics, and politics, in way of life, and in international affairs. For this reason alone the Soviets could command sympathy and support, as did the Nazis half a century earlier, often from the same persons. Many who once turned to Berlin later turned to Moscow as the new citadel of anti-Western power. Soviet colonialism was in areas remote from the Arab lands and in forms unfamiliar to the Arab peoples, who knew only the maritime, liberal, commercial empires of the West. Therefore, to a large extent it escaped notice. Even where such colonialism was intellectually apprehended, it had no emotional impact on the people comparable with that of the Western kind that they had personally experienced. The Turkish experience was different, and so too was the Turkish response.

Despite some impressive achievements in their worldwide competition with the United States, the Soviets were less successful in the Middle East than in most other parts of the Third World. There was no Vietnam or Cambodia in the Middle East, no Cuba or Nicaragua, not even an Angola or a Mozambique. Despite attempts first to browbeat and then to destabilize them, the countries of the northern tier held firm against Soviet pressures, and even the spectacular Soviet gains farther south proved to be limited, precarious, and ultimately useless. Apart from two brief interventions by the U.S. Marines in Lebanon, the Middle East, unlike Southeast Asia and Central America, for a long time required no American troops to defend it against attack or subversion. When finally, in the Gulf War of 1990 to 1991, American troops intervened, it was with Russian support and not against a Russian threat that they did so.

The rollback of the Soviet advance began in Egypt when President Anwar Sadat, after having signed a treaty of alliance with the Soviet Union in 1971, changed his mind and ordered Soviet military personnel to leave the country. Lacking territorial contiguity, the Russians could not respond as they did to acts of insubordination by other "allies"—Hungary in 1956, Czechoslovakia in 1968—by moving in troops and tanks. Instead, they meekly departed. Thereafter, Egypt pursued a more genuinely neutral policy, and when President Sadat decided that the time had come to make peace with Israel, he sought and obtained American encouragement and help in his peace initiative. On that occasion, the Soviets did not help, and failed in their attempt to obstruct the peace process. The lesson was not lost on other Soviet allies in the Arab world, which, while still relying on the Soviet Union as a source of weaponry and generally toeing the Soviet line in international relations, nevertheless began to adopt a somewhat more independent attitude in national and regional affairs. At the same time, the United States, which throughout had retained an imposing diplomatic, economic, and cultural presence in the region, began to pursue more active political and strategic policies and to cultivate, not without success, a number of Arab governments.

This warming up of relations between the Arab governments and the West was accelerated by another development, roughly contemporaneous with the Israel–Egypt peacy treaty—the Iranian revolution of 1979. To the conservative regimes of the Arab world, this appeared to offer a double threat of subversion and invasion and was the more dangerous in that it came not from an alien outsider, but from a Muslim movement within the region that held immense appeal to the downtrodden and the discontented.

The impact of the West in the Arab lands created real problems through the economic, social, and political dislocations to which it gave rise, and the cultural tensions that it engendered. These were in the long run far more important than the various specific political issues as a source of discontent and resentment. They were not, however, easy to formulate and discuss on a political level, especially in countries that had no tradition of such discussion, nor could the blame for them readily be thrown on nameable and recognizable culprits. It was, therefore, the surface political issues that were most to the fore, as both a focus and a manifestation of anti-Western feeling. It was not always easy to tell whether one or another of these issues was an irritant or an outlet—a cause of tension or a relatively harmless way of releasing it. The events of the 1950s and 1960s seemed to show that as the successive veils of political distraction are stripped away, the tension becomes greater and not less.

Saddam Hussein's invasion and annexation of Kuwait in August 1990 confronted the world with its first major crisis since the eclipse of Soviet power and the end of the Cold War. Despite the many difficulties and dangers of the Cold War era, there was a kind of bipolar stability to which both superpowers contributed, the one by maintaining cooperation and the other by imposing discipline among their allies, their satellites, and their protégés. With the abandonment by the Soviet Union of its previous commanding role, this discipline disappeared, and the states on the periphery were no longer primarily influenced in their policies and actions by the fear of punishment or the hope of reward. The United States as the surviving superpower, Europe and Japan as the new economic powers, and the regional powers most directly affected all faced a new situation with little experience to guide them.

The invasion and annexation by Iraq of a peaceful neighbor, a sovereign state, and a fellow member of the United Nations placed that body, and with it the world community, before a terrible dilemma. Should it treat this merely as a local squabble in a notoriously troublesome part of the world, to be resolved if at all by a so-called Arab solution, in which outsiders would be wise not to get involved—or should it see and deal with this as a major challenge to world order and international law, confronting the United Nations with an awesome choice: either to act against Saddam Hussein and restore Kuwaiti sovereignty or to accept the facts and let him have his way? In the Middle East, as elsewhere, those old enough to remember, or wise enough to learn from history, could recall an earlier sequence of events: the Japanese invasion of Manchuria, the Italian invasion of Ethiopia, the German seizure of Austria and then Czechoslovakia. These events led directly to the collapse of the international order and to the outbreak of the Second World War. If Saddam Hussein had been allowed to succeed in his gamble, the United Nations, already devalued, might well have followed the defunct League of Nations into well-deserved ignominy. The world would have belonged to the violent and the ruthless and would have been on the way to universal anarchy or a third world war. The choice gained added urgency from Saddam Hussein's well-known determination to acquire unconventional weapons and his demonstrated willingness to use them, even against his own people.

The choice was for action—to halt aggression and to restore its victim. The successes and failures of Saddam Hussein and his regime in Iraq illustrate two profoundly important changes that had taken place in the Middle East, the second of which is still not fully understood. The crisis followed, and was in part a consequence of, the decline of Soviet power and influence. The aftermath of the crisis revealed, in many different ways, the second change—the self-imposed reduction in the role of the surviving superpower, the United States.

For as far back as living memory can reach, and a while further, the countries of the Middle East were disputed among rival, more developed, outside powers. There were times—as in the great days of the Arab caliphs and the Turkish sultans—when Middle Eastern powers competed for the domination of the known world. But those times are long past, and for many centuries these countries have, variously, enjoyed and endured the attention of outside powers: first the commercial and diplomatic rivalries of mercantilist European states; then the successive clashes of the British, French, and Russian empires, of the Allies and the Axis; and, most recently, the superpower rivalry of the United States and the Soviet Union. In wartime, the Middle East sometimes became the battleground of these powers. In both peace and war, the governments and on occasion the peoples of the Middle East were the object of intensive efforts by outside powers to win their hearts and minds so as to gain access to their communications and resources.

Since the beginning of their careers—indeed, for many countries since the beginning of their national independence—Middle Eastern statesmen have known no other situation, and their foreign policies were in large measure determined by the need to avoid the dangers and, where possible, take advantage of the opportunities of these rivalries. The same, or rather its equivalent, was true of the professional experts in the services of the outside powers whose business it was to deal with these countries. All these now faced a totally transformed situation, in which, for the first time ever, there was only one power, with overwhelming wealth and strength and no real rival to challenge it.

Many misunderstandings arose from the widespread assumption that the United States was an imperial power and the natural successor of Britain and France in the region. But the United States was not an imperial power, and it had neither the interest nor the ambition for such a role. Its purposes in the Middle East had been almost entirely defensive—during the Cold War, to prevent Soviet penetration; in the Gulf crisis of 1990 and 1991, to prevent a stranglehold on a large part of the world's oil resources by a megalomaniac dictator, and the collapse of the world order into anarchy. These purposes having been achieved, the American people, to whom the American government is ultimately responsible, were unlikely to approve any further military involvement in the region.

In the sixteenth century, with the Ottoman conquest of Egypt and the Fertile Crescent and the rise in Iran of a new radical Shīʿite state, the Middle East was once again contested, as it had been in the early centuries of the Christian era, between two rival and expanding powers, one based on the plateau of Iran, the other on the plateau of Anatolia, with its capital in the imperial city by the Bosphorus. The advent of Islam and the expansion of the Arabs from the seventh century had interrupted that process and for a few centuries had reinstated the river valley civilizations of Egypt and Mesopotamia, making them once again, as they had been in a more remote antiquity, the dominant centers of the Middle East. That period, which began with the Arab invasions, ended with the coming of the steppe peoples—first Turks and then Mongols—and the creation of new empires, whose policies and rivalries restored an older pattern.

This, too, was ended by a third wave of conquest and invasion, this time from both ends of Europe. The domination of the European did not equal that of either the Arab or the Turk in its duration or in the range, scope, and depth of the changes that it brought. But while this domination lasted, it had considerable effect, reshaping the political configuration of the region and initiating far-reaching developments, principally in its economic and social life. The period of domination by rival powers and superpowers drew to an end in the last decades of the twentieth century, and it is too soon to judge how deep and how durable these changes will be.

Will the region once again be dominated, as in the days of the Ottomans and Safavids, or of the Byzantines and Sasanids, from the plateaus of Anatolia and Iran? There is much to support such a view: superiority in numbers, in political sophistication, and in virtually all resources other than oil. Or will the peoples of Egypt and the Fertile Crescent succeed in overcoming their differences, realize their potential, and once again restore the power and the glory to these ancient lands? What is new is that now, for the first time in centuries, the course of events in the Middle East is being shaped not by outside but by regional powers—by the governments they form, the policies they choose, the actions they take. The choice, at last, is their own.

Notes

Chapter 1

1. A. T. Mahan, "The Persian Gulf and International Relations," *National Review* (September 1902): 26–45, especially p. 39: "The Middle East, if I may adopt a term which I have not seen...," reprinted in A. T. Mahan, *Retrospect and Prospect* (London, 1903); V. Chirol, *The Middle Eastern Question* (London, 1903), especially pp. 1–6. See also R. H. Davison, "Where Is the Middle East?" *Foreign Affairs* (July 1960): 665–75; and B. Lewis and P. M. Holt, eds., *Historians of the Middle East* (London, 1962), pp. 1–3, where some of these points are discussed.

2. Pliny, *Natural History*, vi.5.

Chapter 2

1. See, for example, R. F. Kreutel and O. Spies, *Leben und Abenteuer des Dolmetschers Osman Aga* (Bonn, 1954), p. 171; and, on the gardens of the Trianon, Yirmi Sekiz Mehmed Efendi, *Paris Sefaretnamesi* (Istanbul, [A.H.] 1302), p. 99.

2. Asim, *Tarih* (Istanbul, n.d.), vol. 1, p. 376, cited in B. Lewis, "The Impact of the French Revolution on Turkey," *Journal of World History* 1 (1953): 118.

3. A. Adnan [Adivar], *La Science chez les Turcs ottomans* (Paris, 1939), p. 57.

4. Muḥammad Iqbāl, *Peyām-i Mashriq* (Lahore, n.d.), p. 255; French translation by Eva Meyerovitch and Mohammad Achena, *Message de l'Orient* (Paris, 1956), p. 189.

Chapter 3

1. Sadullah Pasha, "1878 Paris Ekspozisiyonu," in Ebüzziya Tevfik, *Nümune-i Edebiyat-i Osmaniye*, 1st ed. (Istanbul, [A.H.] 1296); 3rd ed. (Istanbul, [A.H.] 1306), p. 288. In this, Sadullah Pasha is echoing an old dictum recorded by the ninth-century Arabic author Ibn Qutayba and repeated by many subsequent Muslim authors, that "there is no rule without soldiers, no soldiers without money, no money without prosperity, no prosperity without justice and good government." The change in the text is significant. See Ibn Qutayba, *ʿUyūn al-Akhbār*, ed. Carl Brockelmann (Berlin, 1900), vol. 1, p. 26; cf. A. K. S. Lambton, "Justice in the Medieval Persian Theory of Kingship," *Studia Islamica* 17 (1962): 100.

2. W. G. Browne, *Travels in Africa, Egypt, and Syria from the Year 1792 to 1798* (London, 1806), pp. 432–33.

3. Lûtfi, *Tarih* (Istanbul, [A.H.] 1328), vol. 8, p. 15; B. Lewis, *The Emergence of Modern Turkey*, 2nd ed. (London, 1968), p. 112.

4. Sheikh Rifāʿa Rāfiʿ al-Ṭahṭāwī, *Takhlīṣ al-Ibrīz fī Talkhīṣ Bārīz*, 1st ed. (Bulaq, [A.H.] 1265), ed. Mahdī ʿAllām, Aḥmad Badawī, and Anwar Lūqā (Cairo, n.d. [1958]), p. 150; French translation by Anouar Louca, *L'Or de Paris* (Paris, 1988), p. 138.

5. Sadık Rıfat Pasha, *Müntahabat-i Âsâr* (Istanbul, n.d.). Cf. Şerif Mardin, *The Genesis of Young Ottoman Thought* (Princeton, 1962), pp. 169–95; and Lewis, *Emergence*, pp. 132–33.

6. Dufferin to Granville, 6 February 1883, *Parliamentary Papers*, c. 3529, Egypt no. 6, 1883, vol. 83, p. 43.

7. Samuel P. Huntington, *The Third Wave: Democratization in the Late Twentieth Century* (Norman and London, 1991), pp. 266–67.

8. T. E. Lawrence, *The Seven Pillars of Wisdom* (London, 1940), p. 36.

9. Cited in Malcolm H. Kerr, "The Emergence of a Socialist Ideology in Egypt," *Middle East Journal* 16 (1962): 142–43.

10. *Al-Ahrām*, 4 August 1961; French translation in *Orient* 5 (1961): 151–58.

11. B. Berenson, *Aesthetics and History* (1948; New York, 1954).

12. Interview with R. K. Karanjia, 28 September 1958, reported in *Al-Ahrām*, 29 September 1958; English translation in *President Gamal Abdel Nasser's Speeches and Press-Interviews 1958* (Cairo, [1959]), p. 402. The *Protocols* were also featured in an article in the official Egyptian cultural journal: Ṣalāḥ Dasūqī, "Al-Khiṭaṭ al-Ṣahyūniyya fī majāl al-taṭbīq," *Al-Majalla* 4 (November 1960): 7–11; cf. *Al-Majalla* 5 (January 1961): 134–36, where a reader in Damascus, ʿUmar al-Ṭībī, provides additional "information" of the same kind.

Chapter 4

1. Ahmed Refik, ed., "Ali Efendinin Sefaretnamesi...," in *Tarih-i Osmani Encümeni Mecmuası* ([A.H.] 1329), p. 1459; Lewis, *Emergence*, p. 329.

2. Lewis, *Emergence*, pp. 333–40; B. Lewis, *Islam and the West* (New York, 1993), pp. 166–73; Mardin, *Genesis*, pp. 326–36.

3. Mustafa Nihat Özön, *Namık Kemal ve İbret Gazetesi* (İstanbul, 1938), pp. 81–85; cf. Mardin, *Genesis*, p. 327; and Lewis, *Emergence*, pp. 336–37.

4. Sir Lewis Namier, *Vanished Supremacies* (1958; London, 1962), pp. 49, 50.

5. Cited in ibid., pp. 62, 63.

6. U. Heyd, *Foundations of Turkish Nationalism* (London, 1950), p. 43; Lewis, *Emergence*, p. 351.

7. Al-Thaʿālibī, *Fiqh al-Lugha* (Cairo, [A.H.] 1284), p. 3, cited in ʿA. ʿA al-Dūrī, *Al-Judhūr al-taʾrīkhiyya liʾl-qawmiyya al-ʿArabiyya* (Beirut, 1960), p. 46.

8. Midhat Cemal Kuntay, *Sarıklı İhtilâlcı Ali Suavi* (İstanbul, 1946), p. 59; Mardin, *Genesis*, p. 372.

9. Özön, *Namık Kemal*, pp. 263 71, cf. p. 81, Mardin, *Genesis*, pp. 327 38. Lewis, *Emergence*, pp. 332 33.

10. Mehmet Akif [Ersoy], *Hakkın sesleri* (1913), in *Safahat*, 6th ed. (İstanbul, 1963), pp. 205–6.

Chapter 5

1. M. Plessner, "Ist der Zionismus gescheitert?" *Mitteilungsblatt* (Wiener Library, London), no. 42, 24 October 1952.

2. Cited in A. Bausani, "Note su Shah Walīullāh di Delhi (1703–1762)," *Annali dell'Istituto Universitario Orientale di Napoli*, n.s. 10 (1961): 99.

3. Özön, *Namık Kemal*, p. 33, cited in Lewis, *Emergence*, p. 341.

4. Thomas Hope, *Anastasius* (London, 1819; Paris, 1831), vol. 1, pp. 110, 257.

5. Lûtfi, *Tarih* (İstanbul, 1302/1885), vol. 6, p. 51.

6. Cevdet, *Tezakir*, ed. Cavid Baysun (Ankara, 1960), vol. 2, p. 152.

7. Muḥammad ʿAbduh, *Al-ʿUrwa al-Wuthqā* (Cairo, 1957), p. 10, cited in P. J. Vatikiotis, "Muḥammad ʿAbduh and the Quest for a Muslim Humanism," *Arabica* 4 (1957): 62.

8. Muḥammad al-Bahay, *Al-Fikr al-Islāmī al-ḥadīth wa-ṣilatuhu biʾl-istiʿmār al-gharbi* (Cairo, 1957).

9. Liman von Sanders, *Fünf Jahre Türkei* (Berlin, 1920), pp. 330–31; English translation, *Five Years in Turkey* (Annapolis, 1928), p. 312. The Ottoman general Ali Fuat Pasha, in his memoirs, records a similar approach

by Nuri Said late in 1918. See Ali Fuat Cebesoy, *Millî Mücadele Hâtıraları* (Istanbul, 1953), pp. 28–29.

10. Cited in Mahmud Kemal Inal, *Osmanlı devrinde son Sadrıazamlar* (Istanbul, 1940–1953), p. 1892, translated in Lewis, *Emergence*, p. 358.

11. Cited in P. Rondot, *L'Islam et les musulmans d'aujourd'hui* (Paris, 1958), vol. 1, p. 253.

12. W. Cantwell Smith, *Islam in Modern History* (Princeton, 1957), pp. 156–57.

13. Cited in Shaul Bakhash, *The Reign of the Ayatollahs* (New York, 1984), pp. 22, 24, 26, 28, 34.

Chapter 6

1. Cevdet, *Tarih* (Istanbul, [A.H.] 1309), vol. 5, p. 14. See T. Naff, "Reform and the Conduct of Ottoman Diplomacy in the Reign of Selim III, 1780–1807," *Journal of the American Oriental Society* 83 (1963): 310.

2. Cevdet, *Tarih*, vol. 6, pp. 400–401.

3. J. G. McDonald, *My Mission in Israel, 1948–1951* (London, 1951), pp. 181–82.

4. U.S. Department of State, *Nazi–Soviet Relations, 1939–41. Documents from the Archives of the German Foreign Office*, ed. R. J. Sontag and J. S. Beddie. Department of State publication 3023 (Washington, D.C., 1948), p. 259, cf. pp. 244–45, 270.

5. Cantwell Smith, *Islam in Modern History*, p. 159.

Bibliographical Note

There is now a vast literature on the modern Middle East, an increasing proportion of which conforms to accepted scholarly standards. For premodern history, R. Stephen Humphreys, *Islamic History: A Framework for Inquiry*, rev. ed. (Princeton, 1991), provides invaluable methodological and bibliographical guidance. For comparable help in more modern history, the reader must have recourse to a variety of works. A useful and readable general account, as well as a critical guide to the literature, may be found in the two volumes by M. E. Yapp, *The Making of the Modern Middle East, 1792–1923* (London, 1987), and *The Near East Since the First World War* (London, 1991).

Numerous surveys, outlines, and chronologies of events are available in journals and other publications. The best by far over a long period of time is the Italian journal *Oriente Moderno*, published since 1921 by the Istituto per l'Oriente in Rome, and dealing with cultural and religious as well as political, military, and economic matters. An approximately annual analysis of events and developments is provided in *The Middle East Record* (1960–1970), followed by *The Middle East Contemporary Survey* (1976–). Two French publications, *Cahiers de l'Institut de l'Orient Contemporain* (1945–1955) and *Orient* (1957–1969), have unfortunately ceased publication.

The Quarterly Index Islamicus (London) furnishes a comprehensive classified bibliography of current books, articles, and papers on Islamic subjects. Diane Grimwood Jones, Derek Hopwood, and J. D. Pearson, eds., *Arab Islamic Bibliography: The Middle East Library Committee's Guide*

(Hassocks and Atlantic Highlands, 1977), contains much useful material. On more recent issues, George N. Atiyeh, *The Contemporary Middle East, 1948–1973: A Selective and Annotated Bibliography* (Boston, 1975), provides extensive coverage. Among specialized works of reference dealing with the region, mention may be made of the *Encyclopedia of Islam*, 2nd ed., and the *Encyclopedia Iranica*. Both contain numerous articles, with documentation and bibliography, on places, persons, and topics relevant to the modern period.

There are several useful handbooks dealing with different aspects of modern Middle Eastern history. These include Jere L. Bachrach, *A Middle East Studies Handbook*, 2nd ed. (Seattle and London, 1984); Robert Mantran, *Les Grandes Dates de l'Islam* (Paris, 1990); Magali Morsy, *Lexique du monde arabe moderne* (Paris, 1986); Justin McCarthy, *The Arab World, Turkey and the Balkans (1878–1914): A Handbook of Historical Statistics* (Boston, 1982); Lawrence Ziring, *The Middle East: A Political Dictionary* (Santa Barbara, Denver, and Oxford, 1992); and William C. Brice, *An Historical Atlas of Islam* (Leiden, 1981). The structure of Arab and Muslim personal names is explained in Annemarie Schimmel, *Islamic Names* (Edinburgh, 1989), and Jacqueline Sublet, *Le Voile du nom: Essai sur le nom propre arabe* (Paris, 1991).

A considerable body of modern Middle Eastern writing is now available in English and French—scholarly and ideological literature, as well as fiction and poetry, translated from Arabic, Persian, Turkish, and Hebrew. A representative selection from the first three of these languages is presented in Kemal H. Karpat, *Political and Social Thought in the Contemporary Middle East* (London, 1968).

Index

Arabic names are indexed in the form in which they are most familiar in the West. Generally, names from earlier periods are indexed under the given or first name, while more current persons are found under the last name.

171